POSTCOLONIAL L

Texts and Contexts
Series Editors: Gail Ashton and Fiona McCulloch

Texts and Contexts is a series of clear, concise and accessible introductions to key literary fields and concepts. The series provides the literary, critical, historical context for texts and authors in a specific literary area in a way that introduces a range of work in the field and enables further independent study and reading.

Other titles available in the series:
Medieval English Romance in Context, Gail Ashton
Old English Poetry in Context, Phillippa Semper
The Victorian Novel in Context, Grace Moore

POSTCOLONIAL LITERATURES IN CONTEXT

JULIE MULLANEY

continuum

Continuum International Publishing Group

The Tower Building   80 Maiden Lane
11 York Road   Suite 704
London SE1 7NX   New York, NY 10038

www.continuumbooks.com

British Library Cataloguing-in-Publication Data
A catalogue record for this book is available from the British Library.

ISBN: 978-1-8470-6336-6 (hardback)
978-1-8470-6337-3 (paperback)

Library of Congress Cataloging-in-Publication Data
A catalog record for this book is available from the Library of Congress.

Typeset by Newgen Imaging Systems Pvt Ltd, Chennai, India
Printed and bound in Great Britain by
CPI Antony Rowe, Chippenham, Wiltshire

CONTENTS

SERIES EDITORS' PREFACE

Texts and Contexts offers clear and accessible introductions to key literary fields. Each book in the series outlines major historical, social, cultural and literary contexts that impact upon its specified area. It engages contemporary responses to selected texts and authors through a variety of exemplary close readings, by exploring the ideas of seminal theorists and/or a range of critical approaches, as well as examining adaptations and afterlives. Readers are encouraged to make connections and ground further independent study through 'Reading and Research' sections at the end of each chapter which offer selected bibliographies, web resources, open and closed questions, discussion topics and pointers for extended research.

Gail Ashton and Fiona McCulloch

PART ONE

CONTEXTS

CHAPTER ONE

SOCIAL AND CULTURAL CONTEXTS

POSTCOLONIAL LITERATURES AND POSTCOLONIALISM

Postcolonial literatures encompass that complex and various body of writing produced by individuals, communities and nations with distinct histories of colonialism and which diversely treats its origins, impacts and effects in the past and the present. While there is much confusion about the relationship between the term 'colonialism' and the related term, 'imperialism', it is perhaps useful to pause and briefly distinguish them. Colonialism refers to the practice of planting and securing colonies, initially for capital and commercial gain as in the operations of the British East India Company in the eighteenth century, then later as a means of consolidating and expanding the realm of (national) power or sphere of influence. Even the meaning of 'colony' has shifted in time. Initially, it was taken to refer to distinct kinds of farming settlement or plantation, often, but not always in distant locations (Ulster, Nova Scotia, New South Wales), but increasingly it came to refer, with the rise of the European empires in the nineteenth century, to those areas subject to systems of rule or control by the European powers (Howe 2002). Colonialism isn't just or only a European phenomenon but it is a term that is commonly tied to European and North American expressions of 'Imperialism', often defined as the attitudes, structures, philosophies or processes that facilitate the practice of colonialism. Imperialism takes many forms and it is important to remain attentive to how both imperialism and colonialism are variously reconstituted today.

Postcolonial literatures are also often variously termed the 'new literatures (in English)' which accentuates the recentness of their histories, or 'world literatures' which defines their 'global' nature and amplifies the geographic spread of colonialisms, past and present. The origins of 'postcolonial literatures' and 'postcolonial literary studies' are plural and their development is central to the evolution of the interdisciplinary field of 'postcolonialism' or 'postcolonial studies', which refers to the diverse study of postcolonial societies, cultures and identities by scholars from a variety of disciplines in the human and social sciences. The rise of English as a global language tied to its histories as *the* language of the British Empire means that both the language and its literature become a site of contest for the colonized, a means of challenging the political and cultural ideologies of Empire. This is particularly evident in writing from the early twentieth century onwards, when the gradual fracturing of the Empire generates new kinds of assessment of its cultural legacies. So, in the writings of Mulk Raj Anand and Raja Rao, of Wilson Harris and Kamau Braithwaite, of Chinua Achebe and Wole Soyinka, distinct national and regional literatures in English from India, the Caribbean and Africa exploring the specificities of colonial and postcolonial identities emerge, often at different times, often deploying indigenous or hybridized forms and models to contest the primacy of imposed or imported cultural forms.

The emergence of such literatures is tied too to how the discipline of English and the project of Empire were mutually constitutive of each other, and to the diversification of English as an academic discipline in the 1950s and 1960s which resulted in the development of, for example, the study of 'Commonwealth literatures' in universities. This guide is primarily concerned with literatures in English and thus it rarely examines the wide variety of cultural production in other colonial languages (apart from French) or in indigenous languages like Swahili, Hindi or Urdu, except as they appear in English translation. It does however explore the kinds of questions a student of postcolonial literatures might want to ask about the relationship between English and other languages in and after colonialism, and about the forms of cultural and economic power that shape the horizons of reading (including the author's own). This means that the student of postcolonial literatures is encouraged to ask questions about and name the locations from which this writer offers such an introduction and to consider the locations and terms under which they consume or make use of a guide such as this. It might seem an obvious point to make, but all guides are selective, partial; they offer a snapshot of a field of study while providing a distinct set of coordinates for readers seeking orientation in the field.

'Postcolonial literatures' and 'postcolonial studies' have gradually been institutionalized in the academy and in the process of their institutionalization, the focus, emphasis and use of the term 'postcolonial' has thickened and mutated, become the subject of noisy contest as has the field of study itself. Early usage of the term 'post-colonial' (with a hyphen) or 'postcolonial' was, as many scholars have noted, as a periodizing term, deployed by political scientists, economists and historians to describe a particular epoch, usually contiguous with a distinct moment of political Independence. Thus, for example, 'post-colonial India' could be taken to refer to India after 1947, the occasion of Indian Partition and the birth of Pakistan as a new nation. It refers to a moment of significant dismantling of the political and economic architecture of colonialism: of decolonization. However, more commonly, particularly in literary and cultural studies, the term 'postcolonial' addresses itself to the ramifications of colonialism from the point of first contact, to beginnings as well as putative endings. These differences in use or terms of reference encourage us to question what the 'post' in postcolonial stands for. While the 'post' in 'post-colonial' may offer the moment of political independence as a distinct site of departure, may 'imply an end, actual or imminent, to apartheid, partition and occupation' suggesting 'withdrawal, liberation and reunification' (Moore-Gilbert et al. 1997: 2), in fact, deeper examination of colonialisms and their impact reveal their passage to be uneven and longer lasting than such notions of ending suggest. The post in postcolonial thus stresses continuities *and* departures. It refers to what continues in the wake of colonization as what conditions pertain from first contact, to those conditions that are continually transformed and revivified by its powers in the aftermath rather than clearly demarcating the absence or withdrawal of colonial power as such.

This recognition relates to another usage of the term 'postcolonial' where it describes a range of critical practices or approaches employed to understand the various dimensions and ramifications of colonization and its aftermath. Such approaches are informed by the diverse theoretical and critical voices associated with 'postcolonial studies' or the critical field of 'postcolonialism' including Frantz Fanon, Edward Said, Stuart Hall, Gayatri Spivak, Homi Bhabha, Trinh

T. Minh-ha, Helen Tiffin, Aijaz Ahmad, Benita Parry and Partha Chatterjee. Ato Quayson's survey, *Postcolonialism* (2000), bears the sub-heading, 'Theory, Practice or Process?' which implicitly registers both the ambiguity and flexibility of the term (postcolonial/ism) and its key sites of intervention. The editors of *Postcolonial Criticism* (1997), meanwhile, peg the term to a field of political engagement that is 'a site of radical contestation and contestatory radicalism' (Moore-Gilbert et al. 1997). Similarly, Robert Young's portrait of the field, *Postcolonialism: A Short Introduction* (2003) proclaims:

> A lot of people don't like the word postcolonial . . . It disturbs the order of the world. It threatens privilege and power. It refuses to acknowledge the superiority of western cultures. Its radical agenda is to demand equality and well-being for all human beings on this earth. (7)

Here, the 'postcolonial' in 'postcolonialism' names a set of transformative political practices, ideals of social justice and ways of thinking and doing that involve a deeply considered engagement with 'the experience of colonialism and its past and present effects, both at the local level of ex-colonial societies as well as at the level of more general global developments thought to be the after-effect of Empire' (Quayson 2000: 2). While he's certainly not alone in the transformation of the term 'postcolonial' from its earlier usage in naming a historical period or moment, to one that refers to a transformative project, informed by a range of often competing political philosophies and models of activism, nonetheless Edward Said's groundbreaking study, *Orientalism* (1978), is a critical marker in the development of postcolonial literary studies and postcolonial theory.

Said's influential work takes as its central concern, the construction of the Orient as an object of Western investigation and control, and of Orientalism as a 'western style' or 'discourse' for 'dominating, restructuring, and having authority over the Orient' (Said 1978: 3). Said's focus on Orientalism as a 'discourse' is influenced by Michel Foucault's and Antonio Gramsci's explorations of the intimate relations between knowledge and power. In mapping the provenance and operation of such discourse, Said illustrates the extent to which Western systems of scholarship and canons of aesthetic representation, especially since the eighteenth century, are implicated in the wider history and organization of the West's material and political domination of the non-Western world. His study marks an important 'move from the description of the material factors governing empire (economic, bureaucratic) to an analysis of representation and the links these have with the ultimate constitution of imperial and colonial power' (Quayson 2000: 4). Said goes onto develop this concern with representation, notably in *Culture and Imperialism* (1993), and he is a formative figure in the development of colonial discourse analysis, a critical component of early postcolonial literary study (Hulme 1986, Mills 1993). The 'postcolonial' in postcolonial writing thus amplifies the nature of its wider cultural work, how it interrogates the past and present operation of historical forces and dominant ways of reading them that underscore local, national and international identities.

DIASPORAS – OLD AND NEW

Diasporas are a critical site of exploration and debate within postcolonial literatures where they name both 'a *geographical* phenomenon – the traversal of physical terrain by an individual or a group – as well as a theoretical concept: a way of thinking, or of representing the world' (Procter 2007: 151). They constitute a key resource in articulating colonial and postcolonial identities and are dynamic forces of cultural interchange and hybridization. European colonialism in Africa, Asia and the Americas created a range of diasporic formations. The animation of older diasporas and the creation of new ones are a continuing effect of current globalizing forces. The term 'diasporas' describes communities shaped by histories of dispersion and migration between or within continents but for whom an attachment to the homeland, real and imagined, continues to provide a key site of identification, a compelling font of memory (Cohen 2008). Diasporas are thus marked by multiple attachments, to the homeland and host land, and are often further transformed by subsequent histories of movement like the migration of Afro-Caribbean communities to Canada or of Ugandan–Asian communities to Britain. While sometimes unified by a shared ethnic or religious identification, as often diasporas mirror the divides of the homeland, reshuffling them in fertile and violent ways and producing a dizzying range of proximities and intimacies across geographical locations.

The classic use of the term, 'Diaspora', derives from the study of the Jewish experience of dispersion but it has been extended to include the historical experience of other groups like Africans,

Armenians and the Irish who like Jewish peoples often conceived of their movement across the globe as arising from a catastrophic event in their history that has, thereafter, substantially conditioned the life and identity of the community. So, for example, the transatlantic slave trade stands as *the* historical experience that permeates the Afro-Caribbean diaspora just as the Partition of India in 1947 is understood as a foundational moment in the creation of several South Asian diasporas (Indian, Kashmiri, Pakistani). Such events and their traumatic aftermaths assume a power that can overwrite more various experiences in the lives and continuing histories of diasporas. With this in mind, Vijay Mishra's account of Indian diasporas asks us to recognize the differences between old and new diasporas and between forced and voluntary migration in particular. 'Old' diasporas denote those communities that are a product of 'early modern, classic capitalist or, more specifically nineteenth century indenture' that brought, for example, Indian labour to the Caribbean in the aftermath of the abolition of slavery, while the 'new' refers to later capitalist formations, those communities in Australia, Canada, New Zealand, the UK and the USA formed from post 1960s patterns of global migration (Mishra 2007). Clearly, new diasporas are both distinct from yet linked to the old. So, new 'trade' diasporas like those which arise out of current movements from China to Africa with the aim of harnessing its natural resources, are a distinct product of China's current global repositioning but also invoke older patterns of migration like that created by the Australian gold rushes in the 1850s which brought migrants from China to Australia to work in both agriculture and the goldfields. Diasporas are then both *specific*, emergent from a *distinct* set of historical, social and geo-political circumstances and yet also a dynamic, fertile and *recurrent* feature of a world marked by the constant movement of peoples, resources, media, translated by familiar and new circuits of power, like that represented by global capital or the world wide web respectively.

Diasporas are often celebrated as the paradigmatic condition of late modernity and associated with the acceleration of (social) mobility and greater recognition and promotion of processes of (cultural) exchange and transformation. However this is often at the expense of recognizing the extent to which they might herald the continuation of disabling as well as enabling attachments to notions of 'home', 'homeland' or nation. The deeply embedded structures of power and domination that have led to or are the product of the occasion of dispersal are often masked or elided. For some critics, in heralding the possibility of new transnational models of identity and belonging, diasporas seem to prefigure the withering of the nation and of national identity as a defining component of individual and collective identities. However the attractions of transnational affiliations over national ones are often overstated for the appeal of the nation-state (and of a bounded secure national territory) to marginalized, dispossessed or displaced groups remains strong. This is illustrated by the ongoing investments and claims of Kurds, Chechens, Basques, Kashmiris and Palestinians for autonomous states that would realize and protect their material and cultural interests. More recently, post 9/11 and 7/7, diasporic communities have been viewed with renewed interrogation and suspicion. This newly charged attention to the relations between diasporas, their homelands and host lands, is related to the changing use of the term apparent from the 1980s onwards where diaspora is increasingly deployed as ' "a metaphoric designation" to describe *different categories* of people – "expatriates, expellees, political refugees, alien residents, immigrants and ethnic and racial minorities *tout court*" ' (Cohen 2008: 1). Yet, the figure of the exile, the migrant or the stranger has preoccupied the West perpetually and so some forms of continuity clearly exist between the latest expansion of the term to include contemporary perceptions of danger, and those longer tenured fears that permeate the history of Empire.

It is important to distinguish between migrancy and diaspora, even as one gives birth to the other, especially since contemporary migrants are often demonized in moments of national panic, even as other discourses of national identity work to promote the benefits of migrancy and to foster inclusion. In 'Fortress Europe' the obsession with securing Europe's borders even as interior boundaries between countries fall with progressive EU expansion, means that contemporary figurations of the migrant betray a nexus of fears, many of which signal the economic, political, temporal and spatial insecurities of the host land rather than reflecting any actual threat posed by migrants.

If migrancy is most often addressed in terms that stress questions of movement, dislocation and displacement, diasporas are differently but not always distinctly freighted. Historically, they settle in the new place rather than return to homeland. They are 'in place', but because of a tendency to emphasize diaspora as *dislocation*, the question of how diasporas *relocate* is often overlooked (Brah 1996). Of course, for some communities, return to the homeland remains a motivating political or social ideal as is the case with the Jewish and Palestinian diasporas. In this instance, the moment that marks the Jewish return to a homeland, the foundation of Israel in 1948 is also, for the Palestinians, a cataclysmic moment of rupture, remembered today as *al-Nakba* (the catastrophe). For other communities, some patterns of voluntary physical return to the country of origin are facilitated by abrupt or unexpected changes in fortune. The growth of the Irish economy ('Celtic Tiger') in the late twentieth century has led, for example, to the unexpected phenomenon of reverse migration (to Ireland) from historic sites of Irish diaspora (UK, America, Europe) at roughly the same time that the country began to experience greater diversity in its inward migration patterns with progressive EU expansion. Given the severity of the current global economic crisis and its parlous effects on the Irish economy, now seriously constricted, it remains to be seen how permanent such reverse and new migrations will be. Nevertheless, such examples illustrate how diasporic returns can themselves generate and intersect with new displacements and emplacements. As a general rule however, diasporas do not return to the homeland.

Diasporas originate in journey. Nowhere is this more apparent than in the formation of the 'first' African diasporas, in the crucible of the African slave trade, initiated by the forced and voluntary migrations from Africa during the seventh and eight centuries into the Middle East and India. This earlier movement has been superseded in popular memory by the imperial complex of the transatlantic slave trade, the forced movement of African populations to the Americas (North and South) and to the Caribbean. Estimates suggest that around 11–12 million people were brought from Africa to the Americas. The scale and duration of the Indian Ocean and Atlantic slave trades, ranging from the seventh to the nineteenth century, distinguish them from other creations of diaspora, often seen as rooted in singular, more temporally bounded catastrophes, like the Irish Famine (1845–1848). The Atlantic slave trade has a distinctive force in popular memory and it is an important site of discussion in postcolonial literatures, because the places and peoples transformed by its operations (Africa, the Americas, the Caribbean and Britain) articulate a set of distinctive, traumatic and deeply connected experiences forcibly represented in its literatures.

Illustrative of how slavery sunders and connects peoples and places across the globe are the stories of the 'middle passage' itself, of the initial journey from (West) Africa to the Caribbean and Americas. Its most resonant image is the slave ship. Historically, the slave ship is a potent site of diasporic imaginings, resistances and recreation. A potent symbol of the political economy of slavery, it also denotes the destruction of African societies inaugurated by the wrenching of people from place. This dissemination of peoples and culture also gave birth to new forms of cultural reconstruction in its traumatic wake: 'The Middle Passage thus emerges not as a clean break between past and present but as a spatial continuum between Africa and the Americas' (Diedrich et al. 1999: 8).

For Paul Gilroy, the ship is a defining chronotope (space–time image) in exploring 'the black Atlantic', a term devised to encapsulate the transnational affiliations between communities in the Atlantic region resulting from the diasporas created by slavery. Gilroy highlights the role of black presence and black cultural forms in the development of Western modernity and vice versa (Gilroy 1993), addressing longstanding networks of political identification as much as he delineates the trade in people and commodities. Gilroy's 'black Atlantic' offers new routes to understanding the cross pollination of ideas that marks cultural exchanges in these locations, such as that represented by the emergence, in the 1950s and 1960s, of the key architects of black liberation and of a Pan-Africanist politics, devoted to the project of African independence – Aimé Césaire, Marcus Garvey, Frantz Fanon, W.E.B. Dubois, C.L.R. James.

Today, the extraordinary cross pollination of cultural heritages generated is encapsulated in the range of musical genres and forms that owe their genealogy to the fusions of diaspora (jazz, blues, gospel, calypso, ska and reggae to name a few), as much as it is reflected in the literary history of 'the black Atlantic' itself from Olaudah Equiano's *Interesting Narrative of the Life of Olaudah Equiano* (1789) to Toni Morrison's *A Mercy* (2008) or Lawrence Hill's *The Book of Negroes / Someone Knows My Name* (2008). Indeed, the ship continues to link generations brought into new relations by the legacies of slavery. So, for example, the arrival of the 'Empire Windrush' at Tilbury Docks in 1948 and with it a new phase of post-war migration to Britain encompassed a set of departures that distinctively remade British and Caribbean histories. The 'Windrush generation' and their experiences are diversely explored in the work of a range of post-war

'Hulme Millennium Mural' (Hulme Urban Potters), Manchester, UK. Photo taken by Sara Everatt.

and contemporary writers that include Sam Selvon, George Lamming, E.K. Braithwaite, Merle Hodge, Grace Nichols, David Dabydeen, Fred D'Aguiar, Andrea Levy, Bernardine Evaristo and Caryl Phillips.

Such journeys bear within them the memories of those diversely traumatic movements between Africa, the Americas and Britain centuries before. Indeed, boats constitute a resonant image of the multiple forms of journeying that characterize diasporas conjoined or separated in time and space. This can be seen in Amitav Ghosh's plotting of the diverse afterlives of a former slaving vessel, the '*Ibis*', refurbished to exact new forms of trade in the service of the East India Company in *Sea of Poppies* (2008) or the reanimation of the 'coffin ships' of the Irish Famine in Joseph O'Connor's *Star of the Sea* (2004) or the 'convict hulks' and passenger ships that transported Britain's poor and immigrant free labour to Australia, as explored in Anna-Marie Jagose's *Slow Water* (2003) or Kate Grenville's *The Secret River* (2005). More generally, diasporic writing as various as Mourid Barghouti's *I Saw Ramallah* (2004), Jhumpa Lahiri's *Interpreter of Maladies* (1999) and Nam Le's *The Boat* (2008) are preoccupied with those specific ways of seeing and being in the world generated by ongoing forms of displacement and emplacement between communities and continents.

AFRICAN LOCATIONS – WRITING IN THE POSTCOLONY

States of independence

By the end of the Second World War, European colonialisms at the height of their power on the African continent from the mid-nineteenth to the mid-twentieth century were in decline. Three countries were independent in 1945 – Liberia, Ethiopia and Egypt – and between 1945 and 1965, an unprecedented wave of political transformation resulted in the dismantling of European rule across the continent from the North to the South, with Libya, Sudan, Morocco and Tunisia leading the way. In 1957, Ghana became the first sub-Saharan country to achieve Independence and most of the continent followed, so that by the mid-1960s, two thirds of Africa was free with some notable exceptions; the former Lusophone colonies of Angola and Mozambique and present day Zimbabwe (Rhodesia) and Namibia (South West Africa), the latter of which achieved independence in 1980 and 1990 respectively. While South Africa had declared itself a Republic in 1961, its avowed policy of Apartheid from 1948 to 1990 delayed its claims to representative democracy until the first free elections of 1994.

Just as the spread of European colonialism across the continent was often violent and uneven, so the project of decolonization and postcolonial nation building has been erratic and traumatic. The trials of African nations since Independence, often marked by bloody civil wars, military rule, dictatorship, ethnic conflict and genocide, prolonged by continuing social inequalities are critical to an understanding of the urgent social issues facing Africans now. Today, African resources are the subject of renewed competition from without as within and at the vanguard of the new rush for Africa are China and the Middle East. While China seeks the mineral resources to sustain its terrific industrial advancement, the Middle East turns to North Africa in particular as a key source of its future food security. These investments come at a great price for local peoples and ecologies, displaced and reshaped anew by foreign capital which, continuing the legacies of European colonialism, secures the profits from those resources in the hands of a few. At the same time, a large proportion of the local population face resource insecurity (because of the stagnation of agricultural production aimed at supplying Africans), or are dependent on international aid. If, however, civil conflict and competition, or the workings of "necropower" (Mbembe 2001) are the prevailing terms through which we approach Africa since Independence, we overlook and underestimate the plurality and vivacity of contemporary African social realities. In this we need to pay attention to the locations from which we construe Africa.

Locations

So, from where do we configure Africa? How is Africa understood from the economic coordinates of the global North or the global South? How is it located in its European, American or Asian diasporas and by European and Asian diasporas on the continent? Is it more useful to talk of the regional rather than the national in approaching African cultures, to speak of an East African rather than say a Kenyan or Tanzanian identity? What kinds of relationship do different ethnic groups have with/in newly emergent nations in the colonial and postcolonial eras? Given the periodic resurgence of ethnic rivalries between, for example, the Kikuyu and Luo over land distribution in Kenya, what role does ethnicity play in African social formations today? What can be learned from histories of peaceful coexistence as from histories of conflict in African locations? What distinguishes countries with substantial recent histories of white settlement and governance like South Africa and Zimbabwe from other African countries? How do questions of race mark notions of Africanness today?

Such questions, if both numerous and complex in their answering, are nevertheless important because they work to dissolve a historic tendency to think of 'Africa' in the singular and promote instead the recognition of African pluralities, 'Africas'. Examining this creation of a monolithic Africa, Achille Mbembe notes how 'as a name, as an idea, and as an object of academic and public discourse [Africa] has been, and remains, fraught' (Mbembe and Nuttall 2004: 348), not least because it has been continually imagined as a constitutive Other of the Western imagination (Said 1978). As such, Africa is often construed 'as an object *apart from the world*, or as a failed and incomplete example of something else' (Mbembe and Nuttall 2004: 348), most often of the promises of new beginnings that came with African independence from colonial rule. Such readings of Africa distort and underplay its many histories, the diversity of ways in which it is 'in' the world as much as the world is 'in' Africa. African cultures are remarkable for their mixing of cultural influences, traditions and indigenous and European languages, being both polycultural and polylingual. The category 'African literature' includes oral and written literatures in indigenous languages such as Kikuyu, Hausa, Sotho, Xhosa, Somali and Swahili, alongside those African literatures in Arabic, French, Portuguese, Afrikaans and English perhaps more familiar to those outside Africa. Literatures in English are the focus here but they cannot be understood without deeper recognition of the larger cultural hierarchies and social pressures that pervade African locations. For example, social inequalities, linked to poverty and/or the marginalization of nomadic or indigenous communities in particular, continue to condition adversely, access to education, and thus shape life chances and cultural sustainability. Adult literacy figures are widely varying and improving, particularly in East Africa, but adult literacy in the sub-Saharan region currently stands at about 59 per cent, which when set against other demographic trends, suggests an overall increase rather than decrease in adult illiteracy in the region since 1990 (UNESCO 2008: 35). Varying degrees of literacy shape the ways in which people can participate in or are excluded from culture and/or how they gain a purchase on literature as cultural form.

A vibrant oral tradition of storytelling is central to African cultures, and thus the study of African literatures demands an attention to the range of ways in which this orality (or orature) shapes literary expression. Orature is critical to the history of the African novel in English. While the first accredited Nigerian novel in English, Amos Tutuola's *The Palm-Wine Drinkard* (1952), is only some fifty years old, the written word has nevertheless been in Nigeria for at least a thousand years reflecting the diversity of cultural traffic in the region prior to European incursion (Griswold 2000). Recognizing the cosmopolitan nature of African cultures *before* and after colonization foregrounds how writers and storytellers, like the *griots* (poets, praise singers) of West Africa and their audiences, juggle multiple ways of being in a world where Islam, the Christian religions and animist beliefs collide and coexist. Just such a figuration of the African as the product of 'the crossroads of cultures' (Achebe 2006: 143) and belief systems is prevalent in the work of Nigerian writers like Chinua Achebe, Christopher Okigbo, Mabel Segun, Flora Nwapa, Wole Soyinka, and Ben Okri. Retaining a keen sense of how 'Africa' has been produced historically helps us to understand the conditions under which African social formations are renewed and reshaped post-Independence.

Decolonizing the mind

The often bloody struggles of the Independence era shaped the terrain of African literatures in formative ways. The work of the most recognized African writers in English – Chinua Achebe, Wole Soyinka and Ngũgĩ – trace the challenges facing Africans tackling the measure of colonial incursion into culture and the questions of how to decolonize, reform and revivify a national culture. Literature in the immediate post-Independence period set about the task of documenting the varied legacies of colonialism, mapping the coordinates of postcolonial African identities and debating the kinds of cultural values that could and should determine African futures. As Nana Wilson-Tagoe notes:

> For most novelists of the 1960s and 1970s, writing the story of the colonised was either a way of constituting the modern community of the nation or a process of investigating its collapse . . . In most African texts, nation, culture and identity were linked thematically to place and place was seen as the determining context of cultural value. (2006: 96)

In the literature of African independence, that place was often the village, the proposed home of myth and tradition. Indeed, the village, idealized or destabilized, was central to the construction of a common vision of African rural life before and after the colonial encounter. As well, in Southern and East African literature in English and Afrikaans, the settler farm too bears a comparable burden of representation even as it speaks to and about a different set of ideological imperatives.

Central to the question of decolonization are processes of cultural reclaim and renewal that involve a revisiting of the ideologies embedded in the book as a vehicle of culture. The role of the book in Africa as the bearer both of cultural freedoms and imprisonments is a key feature of the interrogation of colonialism and neocolonialism in

African spaces. It is central to Wole Soyinka's dissection of his childhood education in colonial Nigeria, *Aké* (1981). It motivates the interrogation of African and European intercultural exchange in Ama Ata Aidoo's *Our Sister Killjoy* (1977) and Dambudzo Marechera's *The Black Insider* (1990). It is deeply woven into literary representations of colonial and postcolonial incarceration. In all, the centrality of the written word as a tool of resistance and self-preservation is critical. It provides the means to challenge or circumvent state power and to interrogate the ways in which European and American cultural power continues to shape the continent, not least in the ascent of English as a global language. Such interlacings of freedom and imprisonment in an African history of the book might address the smuggling of the manuscript of Ngũgĩ's first novel written in Gikuyu, *Devil on the Cross* (1982) out of a Kenyan prison, Ken Saro-Wiwa's letters protesting his imprisonment for defending the Ogoni peoples, the myriad testimonies detailing South Africa's Apartheid complex like Joyce Sikakane's *A Window on Soweto* (1977) or Nelson Mandela's *Long Walk to Freedom* (1995). Equally, the varied fates of the 'African' book in the world, as epitomized for example, by the promulgation and reception of the Heinemann African Series in Europe, or the relative dominance today of South African writing in English in the 'global imaginary' (de Kock et al. 2004) are central concerns in emergent postcolonial histories of the book in Africa. These map the creation and recreation of African literary canons across time and space and foreground the operation of global as well as internal cultural hierarchies in the constitution of Africanness.

Rural, urban, peri-urban Africas

In much African writing of the post-Independence period, the village is the succour of tradition. As often, it is the site of origin or spiritual retreat from the purported evils of the postcolonial city. 'Once seen', as Achmat Dangor has it, as 'transiently evil, a gigantic asphalt salt mine into which Africans had been thrust after imperial Europe had wrenched them from their rural innocence' (2004: 37), African cities like Johannesburg have long been tainted by their genesis in colonial and neocolonial exploitation and much African fiction, like Maja Mwangi's *Kill Me Quick* (1973) or Ayi Kwei Armah's *The Beautyful Ones Are Not Yet Born* (1968) maps African formations from this perspective. But like many African writers (Ben Okri, Zakes Mda,

Moses Isegawa, Phaswane Mpe, Helon Habila, Yvonne Vera), Dangor seeks to reclaim the urban and peri-urban from its detractors. Africans are increasingly urbanized (38% in 2005) and no continent is urbanizing faster. Africa will have more megacities or large urban centres than any other in the twenty-first century. Today, Cairo, Lagos, Nairobi, Dhaka, Johannesburg and Cape Town are dynamic forces of economic and social change and discrete hubs of interchange. They bring cultures and economies together in innovative ways, giving birth to new forms, languages and ways of being. While the spectacle of the African 'slum' that appears in recent films like *The Constant Gardener* (2005) operates as *the* predominant figure of African metropolitanism, particularly in the West, it greatly simplifies and overlooks the varied and ever changing urban scene that constitutes the African city now, from North to South, East to West.

Women, community and culture

The struggle with the village and its structures in re-defining African womanhood and exploring the often eclipsed role of women in African societies is a key point of departure in the work of early post-Independence writers like Bessie Head, Ama Ata Aidoo, Flora Nwapa, Nawal El-Saadawi, Grace Ogot, Mariama Bâ, Buchi Emecheta and Tsitsi Dangarembga. The interrogation of women's lives in African culture today is continued by newer writers like Promise Okekwe, Pettina Gappah and Sefi Atta. It has also constituted an important subject for African men, in Nuruddin Farah's *From a Crooked Rib* (1970) and in the films of the Senegalese director, Ousmane Sembene, from *Black Girl* (1966) through *Faat Kiné* (2000) and *Moolaadé* (2004), for example. Interrogating how women's lives are shaped in African cultures, men and women conduct a vigorous debate with African *and* Western models of womanhood, particularly motherhood. Such interventions occur in social contexts in which women are consistently the subject of ideological and physical contest. Here we might pause and ask some questions specifically of the social contexts in which African women are located, precisely to bring such contest into view.

What roles do women play in African cultures? What are the most common images of women in literary representations of African culture? How are women shaped by and reshaping anti-colonial and postcolonial nationalisms? How do they negotiate indigenous cultural traditions and norms? In what ways are women positioned in the dominant religions and actively reshaping religion in Africa? In what ways is the veiled African woman located in debates about radicalism, oppression or cultural identity in African and non-African locations? Under what terms is domestic and sexual violence against women normalized in some African locations? What are the effects on African societies of the use of rape as a weapon of war? How do such questions demand a concomitant assessment of African masculinities?

The spread of HIV/AIDS across the continent is a primary social fact that generates particular challenges in African locations where the fight against it is hampered by continuing economic and social inequalities and by the local effects of globalization. For example, traditionally responsible for large-scale internal migration from other parts of Africa and between Southern African countries, mines and the informal economies they generate (in sex work, for example), have created new opportunities for the pandemic to take hold. Yet, if globalization accelerates some of the problems that face African communities, it may also create the resources to tackle AIDS, disseminating greater knowledge and promoting the formation of national and transnational networks and institutions to fight the disease on the ground. AIDS has a tenacious set of meanings and taboos in African locations in no small part due to the devastations it has wrought on African communities, where its impact is always uneven, falling most heavily on the poor, the marginalized and women (Patterson 2007) compounded further by the high incidence of sexual violence in certain locations, notably, South Africa.

POSTCOLONIAL FEMINISMS AND THE NATION (IRELAND AND INDIA)

A slim play from an island in the North Atlantic, *Cathleen Ni Houlihan* (1902), by Irish poet W.B. Yeats, and an epic melodrama from the canon of Indian cinema, Mehboob Khan's *Mother India* (1957), the precursor of contemporary Bollywood cinema, might seem to have little in common. Separated by genre, language and geographical location, they are nevertheless united by a shared valorization of self-sacrifice in service of the nation, imagined as a woman. Thus, they illustrate a set of problems with how nationalisms across the globe cast women. Zillah Eisenstein claims that 'a nation always has "a" gender and "a" race although *the gender is usually not spoken*' (my italics) (Eisenstein 2000: 41). But coming from locations with powerful histories of colonialism, what *Cathleen Ni Houlihan* and *Mother India* suggest, is that the gender of the nation is *usually* 'spoken' in multiple and complex ways. Yeats' 'Poor Old Woman' is a figure for the nation and its promised transfiguration. She articulates nationalist mythologies of blood sacrifice, threading notions of war, masculinity and citizenship in anti-colonial resistance. In Khan's *Mother India*, the figure of woman as nation is distinguished further by the protagonist's motherhood. Battling to raise her sons and work the land to free her family from their indenture to the local moneylender, Khan's protagonist, Radha, secures the future through extraordinary labour. So, in *Cathleen Ni Houlihan*, the nation figured as a woman is revivified by the self-sacrifice of its young men, while in *Mother India* the woman's self-sacrifice gives succour to the image of a heroic post-Independence India. In such formations, women's personal history and identity is elided by their role as emblem or ideal, by an interweaving of the national and the feminine that distorts both (Boland 1995).

This concern with how women embody nation or how the nation is differently embodied as a woman in postcolonial cultural production derives, in part, from a governing interest in mapping and interrogating the contours of power in colonial and postcolonial locations. As structures of domination and control, patriarchy and colonialism share certain features, and postcolonial and feminist critics and theorists find some common ground in excavating the ideologies that lend weight to them. Neither 'feminism' nor 'postcolonialism' are unified projects, rather they are more fruitfully understood as a multiplicity of practices and concerns that intersect, deviate and cross pollinate. While, historically, postcolonial theorists have often been accused of privileging questions of race over gender, equally, feminism's attention to gender at the expense of race has meant that it too has faced criticism for its failures to attend to the complexities of race. This is evinced by the productive critiques of feminisms' imperialist tendencies by critics like Hazel Carby, Chandra Talpade Mohanty, bell hooks, Gayatri Spivak and Aileen Moreton-Robinson. So, for example, Chandra Talpade Mohanty (2003) plots the dangers of Western feminist constructions of the 'third world woman', and of transposing homogenizing models of liberation, devised in Western locations and speaking to their determinants and priorities, to other spaces.

The pursuit of social justice is a clear ambition of the practices and interventions that link feminist postcolonialisms across the globe, delineating in theory and in practice the *changing* configurations of gendered nationalisms. The stippling of gender by race, caste, class, history and sexuality is a key theme in many postcolonial literatures interrogating the hidden histories of the colonial state and the more recent histories of nation-states. Yeats' 'Cathleen' and Khan's 'Mother' model dominant examples of how women's roles are imagined in discourses of nation, however such roles are not fixed, unchanging or unchallenged. The familiar pattern of anti-colonial resistance movements in Ireland, India and beyond is that on achieving independence, and power, they replace the constraints on the women they had strategically lifted in liberation struggles. Prevailing inequalities often receive ballast from interest groups keen to consolidate influence in the postcolonial state. In the Irish Constitution (1937) and its promotion of the domestic sphere as *the* proper site for women's contributions to the welfare of the state, we see a clear demonstration of how Catholicism and Republicanism collude to delimit women's roles. The symbolic elevation of women in the mythology of the nation is often accompanied in Ireland and India by their material subordination in the laws, socio-economic structures, religious or social mores of the new state. In shaping the ideological terrain of revolutionary struggles, actively participating in militant insurgency or the democratic government of new states, women deconstruct the roles offered them in nationalist mythology. Just as often though, women are complicit in the discourses that limit them or other women of different class, caste, race or sexuality in their claims to nation in order to secure other powers or privilege. In postcolonial India, the precise crossing of anti-colonial and post-Independence nationalisms by questions of class, caste, religion and history, preoccupies its many interrogators notably Rajeswari Sunder Rajan and Gayatri Spivak who are keen to explore how women continue to negotiate and shape the structures of power that situate them.

LAND, INDIGENEITY AND QUESTIONS OF SOVEREIGNTY

Land hunger

Land and land rights are a critical site of expectation and conflict between communities the world over. This is particularly so in societies in which expulsion from land and expropriation of its resources are often at the root of continuing material inequalities. Societies with a history of settler colonialism like South Africa, Canada, Australia and Israel, while all differently situated, are cases in point. In post-Apartheid South Africa, the troubled progress of key land reform initiatives, devised to address inequalities between South Africans disenfranchised by Apartheid, is a source of ongoing instability. In Zimbabwe and Kenya too, land redistribution and resettlement have, differently, been the catalyst for the resurgence of longer established conflicts. Outside of these specific locations, 'land hunger' shapes the terrain of conflict in postcolonial societies. It is likely to escalate still further in light of global pressures on world food resources, climate change, rising population levels and the abrasion of natural resources, particularly mineral and water resources. Such prospects, in tandem with the exploration of globalization's impacts and the ongoing effects of importing into former colonies, models of democracy and development grown in other places, are a key site of critical discussion in postcolonial literatures and theory. They constitute a clustering of concerns that have accrued the name, 'green' or 'eco-critical' postcolonialisms.

Ecocritical postcolonialisms

The material and cultural histories of Empire on the ground are subject to new forms of investigation in 'ecocritical' or 'green' approaches to postcolonial literatures. When the European powers moved around the globe in search of new lands and commodities (tea, spices, copper, diamonds, rubber, oil) they brought with them, not only people, but animals and plants, systems of animal husbandry and land cultivation, cartographic and botanical knowledge and practices. These were tools and instruments of colonization with a range of material effects on the lives of indigenous peoples, positive and negative. New forms of indigenous resistance to incursion and national and transnational networks of communication and trade were established but on fundamentally uneven terms. Colonizers reordered the spaces they encountered irrevocably, often destroying and/or displacing indigenous people and practices and/or assimi-lating them into governing regimes (Carter 1987, Bird-Rose 2004). Indigenous peoples, animals, plants and knowledge were requisitioned to service the cultural as well as the economic predilections of the colonizers; Empire gave birth to the human as well as accelerating the spread of the animal zoo, it produced the Great Exhibition (1851) and the ethnographic fair. The legacies of such traffic in people, animals and cultural artefacts are ongoing and complex. They raise important questions about the governing precepts informing colonial rule and expansion and the continuing role of cultural institutions like museums and galleries in shaping the reception of Empire, in reconfiguring colonial and postcolonial national identities.

Green postcolonialisms ask us to reconsider the meaning and effects of past processes and to explore the shape and temper of newer ones. For Graham Huggan and Helen Tiffin, the marriage of shared and differently accented 'utopian' ideals of social transformation in postcolonialism and ecocriticism results in a joint emphasis on unearthing '*conceptual* possibilities for a *material* transformation of the world' (Huggan and Tiffin 2007: 10). The underlying currents of both reiterate that there can be 'no social justice without environmental justice; and without social justice – for *all* ecological beings – no justice at all' (10).

In bringing such awareness to your own locations and encounters with postcolonial literatures and theory, we might consider some of the following questions: What links are there between travels in Empire and the contemporary 'gap year' or 'spring break' in foreign locations? What do the south sea tales of Robert Louis Stevenson and Joseph Conrad have in common with accounts of global tourism like Alex Garland's *The Beach* (1996) or Jamaica Kincaid's *A Small Place* (1988)? How do practices of consumption or trade change across time and space? What does the management of human and animal populations in national reserves like the Masai Mara tell us about how animal conservation policies effect human populations? What uses are made of (indigenous) animals and 'tropical' locations in game shows like *I'm a Celebrity, Get Me Out of Here* or *Survivor*? How are indigenous peoples shaping and engaging conservation discourses in different locations? Who benefits and who loses from discourses and practices of (ecological) conservation? What relationships are there between older and newer forms of maritime piracy? What place do the oceans and the Arctic and Antartica have in histories of imperialism?

Land and freedom

Organized resistances to land displacements which perpetuate inequalities within and between nations, offer some proof that such processes are the site of deep contestation and challenge. The brunt of such movement is often borne by those on the frontline between development, globalization and fragile ecologies – women, indigenous populations and subaltern groups, as Arundhati Roy (2001), Gayatri Spivak (Sharpe 2002) and Vandana Shiva (2002) have shown. Of course, land conflict is shaped by the locations in which it occurs. Indeed, it is the means through which nations consolidate their self-identity, communicate their territorial ambitions and articulate their (border) anxieties and fears as is the case with the wider dispute today between India and Pakistan in relation to the contested territory of Kashmir or between Israel and the Palestinians.

In former 'settler' colonies, the relationship between land, place and (national) identity is conditioned by the fraught histories of encounter between 'settler invader' populations and indigenous or First Nations people. While conflict over land seems particularly visible in former 'settler colonies' like South Africa, Australia, Canada and New Zealand, there are important differences between the examples cited. New Zealand and Canada are to be distinguished from Australia somewhat as the former are marked both by historic land treaties informing subsequent negotiation on issues of self-determination, with evident commitment to some forms of treaty work. Of course, the basis for this in New Zealand's case is the Treaty of Waitangi (1840) which recognized Māori as the holders of certain inalienable rights. This specific recognition continues to condition the terms under which treaty work proceeds (Nicoll 2002).

Indigenous peoples and indigeneity

The forms of devastation delivered by settler colonialism on indigenous peoples, their cultures, lands and languages suggests that 'no other group seems so completely to earn the position of colonized group, so unequivocally to demonstrate the processes of imperialism at work' (Ashcroft et al. 2006: 163). But locating communities in this way can also eclipse their specific engagements with imperial processes and the forms of change, adaptation and reconfiguration at work within indigenous cultures with longstanding participation in global networks of communication and exchange. Indeed the now dominant use of terms like *indigenous, indigeneity* and *indigenous sovereignty* in postcolonial studies, to describe both a particular set of relationships to place and to signal a way of thinking through notions of belonging, indexes a significant change in the approach to colonial and postcolonial settler histories and to the history of representing indigenous cultures.

The use of terms like 'Native American', 'First Nations' or 'San' coined either within indigenous communities or between coalitions of indigenous and non-indigenous, have been a means of opposing the derogatory connotations that earlier terms like 'Indian', 'Eskimo' or 'Bushman' had accrued in settler–invader contexts, and of addressing the reproduction of stereotypical representations of the indigene. Today, the heterogeneity of indigenous peoples is more variously understood. Consolidated by the political mobilization and cultural intervention of indigenous peoples themselves, a greater variety of platforms have emerged for the expression of shared and differing indigenous rights agendas, in the United Nations, for example.

Since their inception, postcolonial literary studies have been preoccupied with and energized by changing notions of the indigene and indigeneity across time and space. They explore the often traumatic history of past encounter between indigenous and non-indigenous settler cultures and its ramifications for contemporary cross-cultural dialogue. At the centre of such debate are indigenous writers and critics whose keen delineation of the role a variety of creative expression plays in the articulation of indigenous identities and experiences is a notable feature of the development of postcolonial literatures. As the terms under which indigenous literature is published, promoted and disseminated in and outside the academy has generated lively debate, so 'the question of who has the right to speak of, about, for Indigenous peoples quickly leads to the question of who or what is "Indigenous" and in what ways "Indigenous" literature [is] distinct from other world literatures' (Damm 1993: 11). Thus, it's worth considering how these questions might be shaped in Latin and South America or India (in discussions among 'tribals' or *adivasi*) or smaller Pacific Rim nations while acknowledging how they demarcate a set of concerns that preoccupy indigenous communities worldwide. Similar movements have generated a greater recognition of Aboriginal and Torres Strait Islanders, Māori, First Nations and San histories of being *in* place in Australia, New Zealand, Canada and South Africa respectively. This has had the effect of making more visible both the violence attendant on settler claims *to* place and the historical privileging of non-indigenous histories of place in the formation and representation of settler identities.

On what terms this recognition takes place and the extent and impact of both symbolic and practical addresses of indigenous rights to place, is, however, much more contentious and embattled terrain. Recent Australian history provides a good example in this respect. Hard-won challenges to the legal fabric of the state resulted in the *Mabo Judgement* (1992), which rescinded the legal fiction that Australia was 'terra nullius' (empty territory) at the time of colonization. The legal possibilities enabled by this positive recognition of indigenous histories of being in place however led the government to quickly dilute and diminish native title rights. Later, the findings of the United Nations Human Rights and Equal Opportunities Commission Report (1997) into the treatment of Australia's 'Stolen Generations' plotted the catastrophic effects on successive generations, of the removal of Aboriginal children from their families in the name of assimilation. The wave of response and cultural debate generated by both Mabo and the 'Stolen Generations' report denote however a shifting of the ground in how many Australians have begun to understand themselves, their past and their relationship to place (Schaffer and Smith 2004). Official and unofficial discourses of 'reconciliation' were newly energized in the aftermath of Mabo but shaken by the 'history wars', the conflicting accounts of the nation's past that it set in motion. The grounds for further engagement and dialogue were boosted by the official public apology to indigenous Australians in 2008, a long denied but important symbolic gesture of national recognition. It remains to be seen if and how such moves can be consolidated by treaty work or/and substantial material improvements in the areas of indigenous health, education and life chance.

Sovereignty speech

Such ambitions are often interestingly focused on the question of sovereignty increasingly central to postcolonial studies where it has generated a body of theoretical work both various and influential, stimulated in no small part, by a range of recent critical interventions including Georgio Agamben's *Homo Sacer: Sovereign Power and Bare Life* (1998), Michael Hardt and Antonio Negri's *Empire* (2000) and the late work of the poststructuralist critic, Jacques Derrida.

Briefly, Hardt and Negri argued for a reading of the contemporary moment as defined by a new, decentralized but increasingly powerful form of sovereignty fired in the supranational regime created by global circuits of production and exchange, between financial institutions, transnational capital and non-governmental organizations. The unfurling of this new 'Empire' across mutable borders is, for Hardt and Negri, facilitated by the parallel decline of old forms of political sovereignty or authority, of the nation-state and the ideologies that sustain it. While this account of the impact of globalizing forces has had considerable influence, it has been repositioned by critical work that elucidates the definite purchase that older notions of sovereignty retain, bound as they are to the idea of a securely bounded territory in which national authority is absolute. Such ideas continue to define ideals of national security from Israel to South Africa to Australia. Rather than passing away as such, national sovereignties are resurgent, newly apparent in the emphasis on border security and with it recurrent border conflicts. A clear embodiment of such force is Israel's longstanding project to build a wall along the entirety of its boundaries. With echoes of the so-called 'peace walls' erected in Northern Ireland during the 'Troubles', this wall is a symbol not just of separation and segregation, but of the precise structuring of power that permeates all encounters between Israeli and Palestinian. In this, it joins a wider catalogue of 'wallings' (Cyprus, Kashmir, US–Mexico border) expressive of the conflicts and contests that impose themselves on the contemporary geopolitical landscape (Sorkin 2005: vi).

Indigenous Sovereignty, while a relatively new term, is one which enters this debate about 'national' versus 'supranational' sovereignty from a different angle as it seeks to encompass the distinctive history of Indigenous ownership, care and custodianship that predates the formation of the nation-states that resulted in the displacement of indigenous peoples. However, the question of recognizing indigenous sovereignty in an Australian context, for example, is seen by its adversaries as a direct challenge to and incompatible with the operation of state sovereignty, partly because distinctive recognition of 'internal' modes of sovereignty are often read as dissolving the 'external' sovereignty of the state. In relation to Australian indigenous political aspirations, it has been argued, by Larissa Behrendt, that it is probably most useful to consider indigenous sovereignty broadly, together with self-determination, as embodying 'a list of claims or a series of tools' (2003: 106) through which indigenous communities negotiate their position in contemporary Australia.

Behrendt offers a critical vocabulary of sovereignty – 'recognition', 'respect', 'control', 'autonomy', 'independent action', 'rights', 'restructuring' – terms which seem on the face of it both familiar and transparent, but which are also site and culture specific.

This vocabulary offers a structure through which we might approach the dynamics of indigenous claims to place and apprehend some of the ways that indigenous histories and identities are embodied. A number of indigenous voices foreground the place of the body and notions of embodiment in the constitution of indigenous sovereignty. In doing so, they make visible how the indigenous body has been located in the prevailing technologies of colonial and neocolonial violence – those interlinked systems of surveillance, discipline and control that have variously taken the shape of the reserve, the mission station or the jail – while refusing the scripts provided by such technologies. For Aileen Moreton-Robinson, '[Indigenous] sovereignty is embodied, it is ontological (our being) and epistemological (our way of knowing), and it is grounded within complex relations derived from the intersubstantiation of ancestral beings, humans and land.' (2007: 2). Such a configuration of sovereignty as the past *and* the present, the human *and* the land, *together*, requires us to consider what we understand by *indigeneity* itself. What does it mean to be indigenous? Here, indigeneity gestures towards distinct forms of self-realization that are 'always placed' (Weavers 2006: 130), relational, the expression of a distinct set of relations with community. As Patricia Monture-Angus suggests, reflecting on Canadian contexts, the question of

> sovereignty (or self-determination) . . . is not about 'ownership' of territory in the way that Canadian politicians and lawyers would define those words. We have a Mohawk word that better describes what we mean by sovereignty and that word is 'tewatatha:wi'. It best translates to 'we carry ourselves'. This Aboriginal definition of sovereignty is about responsibilities and not just rights. (Monture-Angus in Nicoll: 2002).

Here, the imbrication of notions of indigeneity, sovereignty and embodiment are critical in the assertion of self-determination in the 'everyday', a prime site of contest for indigenous peoples given the daily incursions into their self-definition by the continuity and force of non-indigenous visions and attitudes towards the indigene. This focus on the everyday in indigenous sovereignty shares common ground with locations and articulations in diaspora where too a detailed attention to the 'familiar' offers a means to interrogate the longer tenured fascination in postcolonial studies with its opposite, the 'unfamiliar', eccentric, exotic and exceptional (Procter 2006). At the same time, the particular focus in indigenous expressions on how sovereignty is embodied requires us to consider how indigeneity itself might be reconceived as a 'contemporary performance of self that enacts a restoration of relations to one's past' (Nicholls and Murray 2008), resituating and reordering indigenous histories anew.

Such contexts and questions are critical to the study of 'postcolonial' Australian, Canadian, South African or New Zealand writing even as the very existence of such debates makes visible the continuously troubled application of the term 'postcolonial' to describe the experiences of indigenous peoples, many of whom see in the neocolonial actions of the state, proof of the existence of an unbroken chain of expropriation that stretches back to the early days of settlement.

CHAPTER TWO

LITERARY CONTEXTS

THE POSTCOLONIAL *BILDUNGSROMAN*

The prevalence of the *bildungsroman* in the archives of postcolonial literatures has preoccupied critics keen to understand its attractions for postcolonial writers in different locations. With its origins in German aesthetic traditions, the bildungsroman is customarily concerned with the social education and progress ('bildung') of its protagonist. It charts the initiation of the child or young adult into society and the challenges this process generates, often thematized in the protagonist's estrangement from family, community and nation, leading to fraught attempts to renegotiate relationships with place. Stressing the ideological awakening, reformation and assimilation of their protagonists, the genre is inseparable from notions of 'good' citizenship and nationality.

For postcolonial critics, the *bildungsroman* exemplifies the role of the novel in conjoining the histories of nation and empire. The psychological structure of the *bildungsroman* with its emphasis on cultivation, coherence and maturity often forged through the mediating structures of education, lends itself to the creation and reproduction of the justifications for imperialism. For this image of development from child to adult, or evolution from a 'primitive' to a 'fully fledged state of being' motivates and sustains the project of colonialism (Vasquez 2002). Empire like nation depends on the idea of hierarchy, of 'civilized' and 'uncivilized', 'insiders' and 'outsiders', and on the timely assimilation or absorption of its subjects/citizens into the social order to secure its continuity and expansion. It communicates those ambitions in filial terms; it is reliant on the parent–child metaphor in articulating the relationship between colonizer and colonized.

Thus the fledgling colony or newly colonized are often positioned, like the child in the *bildungsroman*, as the unruly subject of Empire's disciplinary regimes and whether those regimes take the shape of school, hospital, prison, reserve, plantation, their governing ideal is the assimilation or reformation of the colonized into the colonial order.

From James Joyce's *Portrait of the Artist as a Young Man* (1916) and Mulk Raj Anand's *Untouchable* (1935) to Randolph Stow's *The Merry-Go-Round in the Sea* (1965), Merle Hodge's *Crick Crack, Monkey* (1970) and Tsitsi Dangerembga's *Nervous Conditions* (1988), the postcolonial *bildungsroman* excavates the role of education in the orchestration of Empire. Such novels explore how education is a vehicle of colonial power, situating Europe and European culture as the repository of value, civilization and history. Education was deemed instrumental to the successful governance of Empire as Thomas Macaulay's 'Minute on Indian Education' (1835) illustrates. In considering how Britain might effectively administer India, Macaulay extols the superior values of the English language and the canon of English literature in creating 'a class who may be interpreters between us and the millions whom we govern; a class of persons, Indian in blood and colour, but English in taste, in opinions, in morals, and in intellect' (Ashcroft et al. 2006: 375). Such ideas devalue indigenous cultures. In order to promote English literature Macaulay dismisses other literatures like Sanskrit and Arabic. In addition, the internalization of the values of the colonizer inherent in such processes can enact a damaging split in the subjectivity of the colonized, reshaping how they think about themselves and their culture (Fanon 1967). This can generate alienation and ambivalence, sources of confusion, hurt and marginalization. Sometimes alienation and ambivalence can also be effective sites of 'speaking back', of resistance to the operation of colonial power. Thus the forms of 'mimicry' that Macaulay sees as necessary to successful governance can also be a means of contesting colonial authority. Attending to how mimicry can be transformative and disruptive (Bhabha 1994) is helpful in thinking about the attractions of the *bildungsroman* to postcolonial writers who variously rework it so that it speaks to their own locations. They thus take possession of it in original ways, refashioning its politics, temper and mobility as a genre.

Postcolonial writers turn to the genre because its focus on *process* and *progress* provide useful tools with which to deconstruct imperialism and its underlying ideals. In so doing the form of the traditional *bildungsroman* is altered and its limitations, like its dependence on the idea of a coherent social order into which the individual is amalgamated, are exposed. So, for example, the estrangements of the 'postcolonial' *bildungsroman* often lead not to the eventual assimilation of the novel's protagonist into the social order, but repudiation and greater exposition of the forms of domination underlying social norms or codes. Indeed the very idea of a stable social order is found to be a regulatory fiction in these writers' excavation of how societies are fractured, damaged and derailed by the legacies of colonialism or the competition or conflict between different political formations in the postcolonial state. Such strategies make the coercive structures of colonialism visible and depict the struggles of the colonized in negotiating the prescriptions of Empire.

Because it is focused on processes of self-formation, on subjectivity, the genre attracts writers keen to explore the trajectory of (national) self-formation in postcolonial locations. In writing set in the early days of the newly independent nation, the struggles of the young protagonist are often linked with wider efforts at decolonizing and the difficulties of establishing the coordinates of a viable post-independence identity. This feature is shared with other forms of postcolonial writing and has been the subject of much critical debate in postcolonial criticism and theory.

In 'Third World Literature and the Era of Multinational Capital' (1986) for example, Fredric Jameson proposes that 'all third world texts are necessarily . . . and in a very specific way . . . *to be read* as national allegories' noting how 'the story of the private individual destiny is always an allegory of the embattled situation of public third-world culture and society' (Jameson 1986: 69). For Jameson's critics, notably Aijaz Ahmad (1992), this statement illustrates a damaging universalism, redolent of earlier colonialist attitudes like Macaulay's. Jameson defends the terms 'first world' and 'third world' as critically useful in understanding the structures of power in the contemporary world. At the same time, he recognizes that such terms eclipse 'profound differences between a whole range of non-Western countries and situations (1986: 67). Even so, his account is seen by Ahmad, as part and parcel of a damaging 'rhetoric of otherness'. Jameson is understood as arguing that 'third world' texts *should* be read primarily as national allegory, as fundamentally preoccupied by the nation as a meaningful political value, and by nationalisms that seem in 'first-world wisdom' (Jameson 1986: 65) both troublesome and regressive. Other critics argue that Jameson's account is less an assertion of what 'the third world' text *is* or an avowal of how the 'third world' *seems* to the 'first', but rather an attempt to describe the ways in which 'global conditions ensure that Third World texts are read allegorically by First World readers' (McGonegal 2005: 258). Jameson's essay remains, for many, a strategically important rehearsal of how literatures are mediated between locations and of the continuing valency of "nationness"' in postcolonial literatures.

The postcolonial *bildungsroman* is one of the many cultural forms where the promises and disappointments of the nation as a political and social ideal across the globe can be productively illustrated. In making visible the structures and politics of the form through both repetition and repudiation of its codes, the continuities and differences between national formations in postcolonial locations are productively juxtaposed. Here, both Hisham Matar's *In the Country of Men* (2006) and Chimamanda Ngozi Adichie's *Purple Hibiscus* (2004) are instructive recent examples. Their plotting of the post-Independence histories of Libya and Nigeria through the viewpoints of their child and teenage protagonists illustrates the multiple forms of investment in the idea of nation as well as its dangers. They map the congruencies between certain forms of post-colonial nationalism and colonialism; the shared technologies of violence (censorship, abuse, torture, war) mobilized in sustaining restrictive ideals of order, progress and national good. In both, the notion of home/land as a defining ideal or destination is consistently put to question, at once making visible how home or nation expresses and maintains its powerful appeal, laying bare its coercive apparatus.

THE CANON AND POSTCOLONIAL LITERATURES

English literature and empire

The emergence of the academic study of English as a distinct discipline coincides with the expansion of Empire in the nineteenth century and the need, on the part of the colonizer, to find a common language through which to rule and unite the spaces of Empire. In this, language is an instrument of conquest and literature its repertoire. The subsequent privileging of English, its institutionalizing as *the* language of Empire, suggests that Empire and the development and study of English literature were mutually constitutive of each other. As Gauri Viswanathan notes, 'the discipline in England took on a shape and an ideological content in the colonial context' (Ashcroft et al. 2006: 376).

So the 'canon' doesn't just refer to a select set of texts (Shakespeare, Milton, Austen, Dickens, Woolf) but how they are invested with cultural authority; the values, attitudes and ways of seeing the world that inform the canon's composition and translation as an archive of 'culture', 'civilization' and 'value'. Gayatri Spivak reiterates this point when she argues: 'It should not be possible to read nineteenth-century British literature without remembering that imperialism, understood as England's social mission, was a crucial part of the representation of England to the English' (Spivak 1985: 243). Spivak foregrounds the dual role of literature as a conduit of imperialism and as a critical component in national self-formation. The canon is shaped by and shaping of the locations in which it is distributed. Thus its reception is often uneven and changeable, in accordance with the time, space and manner in which it is disseminated and the responses of its audiences. Nevertheless, postcolonial writing from different locations shares a number of characteristic features in its address of the canon.

Postcolonial writers explore the canon as a vehicle of culture, excavating the different ways in which it translates the culture of the colonized and pitches the relationship between colonizer and colonized. Thus, for example, Chinua Achebe in 'An Image of Africa' (1977) investigates how Joseph Conrad's *Heart of Darkness* (1901) projects an image of Africa as ' "the other world", the antithesis of Europe and therefore of civilization' (Achebe 1997: 114). He considers the impact of the long tenured 'need in Western psychology' to 'set Africa up as a foil to Europe, as a place of negations' (114) in plotting the denigration of African culture and the dehumanization of Africans he finds in Conrad. Indeed, both distress and unease at how the canon of English literature represents other cultures informs the emergence of postcolonial literatures. Achebe, in an earlier essay, 'The Novelist as Teacher' (1964), situates *Things Fall Apart* (1958), as driven in part by a desire to redress the effects of such representations. However, like many writers he is also motivated by the desire to express the actualities of his own (Igbo) culture, history and environment, to assert his own voice and experience of the world. In this his work is an example of how postcolonial writing, in its articulation of difference and the particularities of place, works to contest *and* reconfigure the canon, decentring and dislocating its claims to universality.

Similarly, Peter Carey's *Jack Maggs* (1997) and Lloyd Jones *Mister Pip* (2006) respond to Charles Dickens' *Great Expectations* (1860) but also to the cultural authority that Dickens and experiences of reading Dickens have accrued. In doing so, they draw attention both to what and how the canonical text excludes and analyse the terms under which it includes others. While Achebe's encounter with Conrad highlights forms of personal and collective damage, the canon can also productively enable or open up other reflections on experience, culture, history and it is important to remain alive to how the canon operates as a site of possession as well as dispossession. The Caribbean poet, Claire Harris, exploring the contradictions of her early education in Trinidad, documents the pervasive racism she experienced in a school designed 'to produce a fully colonised subject' (Williams 2000: 42), but insists that such realities must 'stand with and against' their other side, 'the Classics, Choral Speech, Plain Chant, and Scripture'. Thus she concludes that one of the positive outcomes of the experience was that it generated 'an indelible sense of great beauty, of possibility in language, even as it provided a theatre to observe human nature trapped in a struggle between worldly social and cultural attitudes and evils' (42).

If conversations with the canon are a plentiful feature in postcolonial writing, there are also some common pitfalls to consider in approaching such dialogue. The canon is not homogenous or unified in its organization or understanding of Empire; in this it reflects the ambivalences of colonial discourse. Similarly, it would be a mistake to universalize responses to the canon as always or inherently 'counter canonical' for that underestimates both the motility of the canon and the variety of responses to it. Equally, postcolonial literatures are not wholly preoccupied by canon work, nor is it to be understood as their primary value. To do so, would be to install a damaging hierarchy in which the canonical text is always situated as anterior, the 'original' to the postcolonial 'copy'. The Caribbean poet and painter, Derek Walcott, usefully develops this point in discussing his long poem *Omeros* (1990). Refuting a reading of *Omeros* as a deliberate translocation or translation of Homeric epic from the Aegean to the Caribbean, he argues, rather, that Homer appears as an 'evocation' or a 'series of associations', a 'memory' in the poem. In asserting the distinction, Walcott seeks to underline the dangers in positioning the postcolonial text and the world it constructs as derivative, borrowed, for it divests his Caribbean fishermen of their autonomous reality and culture, the uniqueness of their place (Walcott 2008). So, defining the postcolonial text by its relationship to the canon can re-centre the canonical text and limit understandings of how postcolonial writing is original and autonomous. Indeed, it would overlook how postcolonial writing can illustrate and deconstruct the precarious foundations on which such structures of thought (centre and margin) are built. As Trinh T. Minh-Ha observes: 'The center itself is 'marginal . . . [H]ow possible is it to undertake a process of decentralization without being made aware of the margins within the center and the centers within the margin?' (Ashcroft et al. 2006: 197).

Such recognitions can help us ask questions about the terms in which other canons are formed. Out of our questioning of the canon in Empire another set of inquiries arises, namely about the emergence of 'postcolonial' literary canons and how they are constructed and contested.

Postcolonial canons

If the history of the canon in Empire has led postcolonial writers to consider the ways in which Empire is mediated in 'English literature' and how Empire writing translates the cultures of the colonized, it has also generated a wider attention to the question of translation. Indeed, postcolonial literatures are marked by a sustained attention to translation both as *practice* (from one language to another) and as *metaphor* (as a way of speaking about identity, culture, experience). A key feature of much postcolonial writing has been an attention to the question of the legitimacy and authenticity of the languages of the colonizers (English, French, Spanish) as a means through which to transmit and translate the history, identity and experience of the formerly colonized.

The question of what language/s in which to write has been a dynamic site of contest not least because of the cultural power accrued by colonial languages over indigenous languages like Hindi, Swahili or Irish. This has had distinct effects on the 'memory-bank' of colonial and postcolonial societies. In some locations, their dominance is at the expense of the survival of indigenous languages. In Australia, for example, many Aboriginal languages were lost as a result of the destruction of indigenous cultural pathways and traditions. So, in some cases, language recuperation, even if it is desired, is impossible. Indigenous languages were changed by their encounter with English as English has in turn been transformed by its encounters with other languages. New languages were born out of the intercultural mix of Empire. 'Pidgins', 'creoles' and 'patois', for example, are the product of the meeting of languages in the crucible of colonization and diaspora. The introduction of English in multiple locations at different times means it has also been indigenized and assimilated in diverse ways. As Salman Rushdie observes, English is now one of many Indian languages alongside Hindi, Urdu, Tamil, Marathi, Bengali, but it is one which retains significant economic, cultural and, ultimately, class power as a result of how contemporary globalizing processes consolidate its location as the international language of business or science (Rushdie 1997).

Those same globalizing processes condition the traffic in postcolonial literatures across the globe, shaping what finds its way into local or online bookshops or onto postcolonial literature syllabi. Literature is one of the most powerful mediums through which we access other localities. Cultural institutions such as universities, libraries, publishing houses, national and transnational book prizes (Man Booker, IMPAC) play formative roles in shaping that access; in the selection, dissemination and reproduction of postcolonial literary canons. Reading groups and book clubs (Oprah, Richard & Judy), book 'blogs' (dovegreyreader, librarything) and social networking sites (Facebook, Twitter), the advent of 'google book', e-books and portable digital book readers (including some that even look like books!) are continually reforming reading communities and how, what and where we read. Such movements raise perennial questions regarding the composition and constituency of postcolonial literatures. So we might ask: Who has access to these resources? How do they intervene in the translation of other localities and experiences? How are postcolonial literatures marketed? How are distinct audiences and genres of writing recognized or marginalized in the publishing of postcolonial literatures? How do you account for multiple language communities in your understanding of how texts travel within and between languages? What happens to indigenous language publishing with the ascent of English language publishing? What factors might shape bilingual or multilingual readers' reading choices? Will Vikram Seth's *A Suitable Boy* (1993), first published in English, but lately published in Hindi now be read by more people in its Hindi translation and if so, with what effects? To what extent do popular writers in Hindi, like the late Shivani (Gaura Pant), have the same opportunities to be translated and distributed in English or Tamil or Mandarin?

Such concerns illustrate how postcolonial literatures are embedded *in* and actively engaged *with* global structures and processes of production and consumption. So considering the marketing of a novel or exploring the 'canonizing' processes through which it passes to its readerships is a critical indicator of the terrain of its engagements.

For example, a notable feature of *Mister Pip*'s recent translation to a UK audience was the emphasis placed on the potentially exciting discovery that Jones represented, although an already well established author in New Zealand. Here the idea of discovery emphasized in the publisher's note that the novel was the author's 'first to be published in the UK', insists on its novelty and on the transformative potential this previously denied encounter could offer UK readers. This is reiterated in the defining tagline on the book's front cover – 'A book can change your life for ever' – endorsing also the novel's affirmative encounter with the discoveries, pleasures and possibilities of reading. This focus on discovery could be seen as reiterating the novel's attractions as exotica, resonant in the design, motifs (of flora and fauna), and the colours that populate the hardback cover and its many variations, configuring the book as a desirable object of 'other' worldliness. Such renditions are a common feature of Western representation of Polynesian cultures historically and the chain of reference continues in the emphasis, on the cover, of the novel's 'remote South Pacific island' setting, begging the question, remote to or for whom? Such features may continue rather than challenge dominant perceptions of the South Pacific or may even be productively dislocated by the novel's subsequent account of island life. The cumulative effect of such features however, is that they foreground the relationship between reading, consumption, location and cultural power in specific ways. They demand that we denaturalize reading, excavate how *processes* of reading as well as writing require a deeper understanding of those positions and locations that occasion and inform our reading practices.

BODIES OF EVIDENCE – HISTORIES AND THE POSTCOLONIAL DETECTIVE

Postcolonial writing commonly addresses colonial and postcolonial historiography, the structures, ways of seeing, and critical practices that pertain to the production of history across time and in space. As such, postcolonial writing declares an interest in both 'history', the re/construction of past events, experiences, structures and 'metahistory', the analysis of processes of historical inquiry informing the 'writing' of history. These are conjoined by the image and idea of the archive, an important site of transit in postcolonial writing and theory which unfolds the selective, contradictory and powerful technologies embedded in the construction and maintenance of the archive as a repository of knowledge (Said 1978, Derrida 1998, Spivak 1999, Veracini 2008). In this, postcolonial literatures often make distinctive and strategic use of diverse forms and genres of writing that traditionally organize and disseminate knowledge of the colonized and the colonizer – letters, maps, explorers' journals, travellers' tales, diaries, conduct books, ships' logs and other administrative records – precisely in order to foreground and interrogate the diverse textuality of Empire. So, for example, Daphne Marlatt's *Ana Historic* (1988) offers a *bricolage* of letters, diaries, shipping records, newspaper stories in her imagination of three generations of women in the histories of Canadian settlement, while Richard Flanagan's *Gould's Book of Fish* (2001), subtitled 'A Novel in Twelve Fish', inspired by the paintings of the Tasmanian convict artist, W.B. Gould, offers both a critical account of the visual history of Empire and the material conditions of its production and dissemination.

In revisiting a range of historical events and developments and rewriting them, postcolonial literatures often delineate the forms of interruption that colonialism represents in the lives, histories and experiences of the colonized. In doing so, writers like Michael Ondaatje, Salman Rushdie, Nayantara Sahgal and Peter Carey make particular use of historical metafiction (Hutcheon 1988) in examining the fictionality of 'History' and establishing fiction as an alternative site for the re/construction of histories. Postcolonial writing pays particular attention to vernacular archives (sculpture, rock painting, music and theatre, architecture, orature) in exploring indigenous histories and cultural experiences. These vernacular archives are often transformed by colonial encounter, surviving and adapting to function as powerful mobile resources of self-expression and cultural renewal. So, for example, Patricia Grace explores the Māori 'wharekai' (meeting house) as a resilient archive of Māori knowledge, culture and history in *Dogside Story* (2001). Equally, the Indian writer, Amit Chaudhuri, plots the histories of the musical form, the *raag*, in his short novel, *Afternoon Raag* (1993), in illustrating the 'palimpsest-like texture of Northern India, with its many dyes and hues, its absence of written texts and its peculiar memory' (2001: 258–9). Often, however, indigenous cultural forms don't survive the force of colonial encounter or that of their neocolonial avatars, so Damon Galgut's *The Imposter* (2008) maps the fate of a series of indigenous rock paintings, whose discovery and eventual destruction become a potent metaphor for the continuing corruptions and complicities that mark the 'new' as well as the 'old' South Africa.

In this mode, writing is a kind of archaeology, sifting through the remains of 'History', excavating and resituating those fragmented, local, subjugated 'histories' or knowledges buried by 'History's' total-izing impulses, its appearances as 'Truth'. Such writing, we might, after the work of the French historian and philosopher, Michel Foucault, call 'genealogical' and it is a prevalent mode in the work of a range of postcolonial writers including Wilson Harris, Derek Walcott, Eavan Boland, Robert Kroetsch, Michael Ondaatje and Alex Miller, to name a few. Genealogy, as Foucault reveals it, in 'Nietzsche, Genealogy, History' (1971) 'operates on a field of entangled and confused parchments, on documents that have been scratched over and recopied many times' (Rabinow 1984: 76). It rediscovers past struggles, emphasizing not the smooth passage of cause and effect but rupture, discontinuity, contingency:

> Genealogy does not pretend to go back in time to restore an unbroken continuity . . . On the contrary, to follow the complex course of descent is to maintain passing events in their proper dispersion . . . the accidents, the minute deviations – or conversely, the complete reversals – the errors, the false appraisals, and the faulty calculations that give birth to those things that continue to exist and have value for us. (81)

The 'historical sense' that informs genealogy is heterogeneous rather than homogenous, it makes visible the coerced unity of a 'suprahistorical perspective' (86), it 'refuses the certainty of abso-lutes' (87), it makes visible its own time and place, it doesn't efface its positionality.

Postcolonial writing thus explores 'History' as 'story'; demands that we pay attention to how imperial history organizes, inscribes and sanctifies itself as a sequential narrative, an orderly progress of cause and effect, before and after. As Derek Walcott observes:

> In the history books the discoverer sets a shod foot on virgin sand, kneels, and the savage also kneels from his bushes in awe. Such images are stamped on the colonial memory, such heresy as the world's becoming holy from Crusoe's footprint or the imprint of Columbus's knee. (Walcott 1998: 41)

J.M. Coetzee's *Foe* (1986) and Thomas King's *One Good Story, That One* (1993) excavate the forms of 'heresy' such foundational images of 'virgin sand' and 'kneeling savage' generate in their respective 'writing back' to the foundational images of Empire. 'Writing back' is itself codified in *The Empire Writes Back* (1989) as a key strategy in contesting those totalizing narratives of history that Walcott describes: narratives which explicitly occlude or overwrite the experience of the colonized. Thus, postcolonial writing often counters the homogenizing tendencies of colonial historiography in its attention to the specificities of indigenous histories and place.

In 'writing back' postcolonial writers open up dominant narratives of colonialism, anti-colonial resistance and postcolonial nation building to new kinds of scrutiny and are both various and complex in their rendering of such actions. They both 'return' to history and explore the 'returns' history makes in the present; they map its dispossession and dislocations and crucially refigure possession. Here, postcolonial literatures and theory convene around the figure of the ghost and the shadow, are variously preoccupied by hauntings and the uncanny effects of colonial relations. In this respect, the genre of the gothic offers postcolonial writers a particularly apt mode through which to explore the troubled relationship between history, memory and place.

Postcolonial literatures are marked by their attention to the geographic as well as the historic, the spatial as well as the temporal dimensions of Empire which often congregate in the figure of the map itself. Cartography and colonialism are interwoven. 'Maps are not merely pictures of the world, but depict a world that can be shaped, manipulated, acted upon' (Hall 1992: 383). They are thus expressions and translations of power, organizing and disseminating the values and worldviews of their makers. Maps are thus a potent site of literary intervention and interrogation. The prevalence of the map topos' in postcolonial writing documented by Graham Huggan attests to the clear links between 'a de/reconstructive reading of maps and a revisioning of the history of European colonialism' (Huggan in Ashcroft et al. 2006: 355).

READING AND RESEARCH (SOME DIRECTIONS)

Postcolonial studies and postcolonialisms

- Bill Ashcroft et al., *The Postcolonial Studies Reader* (2006) [Second Edition]
- Robert Young, *Postcolonialism: An Historical Introduction* (2001)
- David Theo Goldberg and Ato Quayson, *Relocating Postcolonialism* (2002)
- Joanne Sharp, *Geographies of Postcolonialism* (2009)

Postcolonial literatures (area surveys)

- Elleke Boehmer, *Colonial and Postcolonial Literature: Migrant Metaphors* (2005)
- Lynn Innes, *A History of Black and Asian Writing in Britain* (2002) and, *The Cambridge Introduction to Postcolonial Literatures in English* (2007)
- Priyamvada Gopal, *The Indian English Novel: Nation, History and Narration* (2009)
- Elizabeth Webby (ed.), *The Cambridge Companion to Australian Writing* (2008)
- Michelle Keown, *Pacific Islands Writing: The Postcolonial Literatures of Aotearoa/New Zealand and Oceania* (2007)
- Alison Donnell and Sarah Lawson Welsh (eds), *The Routledge Reader in Caribbean Literatures* (1996)
- Eva-Marie Kröller, *The Cambridge Companion to Canadian Literature* (2004)

Diasporas (some other fiction, poetry, drama)

- Bernardine Evaristo, *Lara* (1997) and *Blonde Roots* (2008)
- Hanif Kureishi, *The Black Album* (1995)
- Eavan Boland, *Collected Poems* (2005)

- Jhumpa Lahiri, *Unaccustomed Earth* (2008)
- Karlo Mila, *Dream Fish Floating* (2005)
- Grace Nichols, *The Fat Black Woman's Poems* (1984)
- Tom Murphy, *A Whistle in the Dark* (1961) and *The House* (2000)
- Kwame Kwei-Armeh, *Statement of Regret* (2007)
- Hiromi Goto, *Chorus of Mushrooms* (1994)
- Dionne Brand, *In Another Place, Not Here* (1996)

Diasporas (theory and criticism)

- Jana Evans Braziel and Anita Mannur, *Theorizing Diaspora: A Reader* (2003)
- Paul Gilroy, *The Black Atlantic: Modernity and Double Consciousness* (1993) and *After Empire: Multiculture or Postcolonial Melancholia* (2004)
- Homi K. Bhabha, *Nation and Narration* (1990) and *The Location of Culture* (1994)
- Vijay Mishra, *Literature of the Indian Diaspora: Theorizing the Diasporic Imaginary* (2007)
- Ien Ang, *On Not Being Chinese: Living Between Asia and the West* (2001)
- James Procter, *Dwelling Places: Postwar Black British Writing* (2003)
- John McLeod, *Postcolonial London: Rewriting the Metropolis* (2004)
- Aidan Arrowsmith, *Fantasy Ireland: Irish Diaspora Writing* (2009)
- Lisa Lowe, *Immigrant Acts: On Asian-American Cultural Politics* (1996)

African locations

- Chinua Achebe, *Hopes and Impediments: Selected Essays* and *Home and Exile* (2003)
- Wole Soyinka, *Myth, Literature and the African World* (1976)
- Ngũgĩ Wa Thiong'o, *Decolonising the Mind: The Politics of Language in African Literature* (1981)
- F. Abiola Irele, *The African Imagination: Literature in Africa and the Black Diaspora* (2001)

- Tejumolo Olaniyan and Ato Quayson (eds), *African Literature: An Anthology of Criticism and Theory* (2007)
- Kwame Anthony Appiah, *In My Father's House: Africa in the Philosophy of Culture* (1992)
- Achille Mbembe, *On the Postcolony* (2001)
- Michael Chapman, *Southern African Literatures* (1996)
- Stephanie Newell, *West African Literatures – Ways of Reading* (2006)
- Amandinha Lihamba et al., *Women Writing Africa* (2007)
- Simon Gikandi, *The Columbia Guide to East African Literature in English Since 1945* (2007)

Web resources

- http://www-sul.stanford.edu/depts/ssrg/africa/guide.html [Africa South of the Sahara – Online Bibliography of research resources]
- http://www.african-writing.com [British-based online journal devoted to contemporary African writing]

Land, indigeneity, sovereignty (some writers to read)

- Thomas King
- Jeanette Armstrong
- Eden Robinson
- Lee Maracle
- Hone Tuwhare
- Witi Ihimaera
- Oodgeroo
- Jack Davis
- Mudrooroo
- Alexis Wright
- Jackie and Rita Huggins
- Ruby Langford Ginibi
- Kim Scott

Land, indigeneity and questions of sovereignty (some places to begin)

- Jeanette Armstong (ed.), *Looking at the Words of Our People: First Nations Analysis of Literature* (1993)

- Mudrooroo, *Us Mob: History, Culture, Struggle – An Introduction to Indigenous Australia* (1995)
- Jackie Huggins, *Sister Girl* (1998)
- Aileen Moreton-Robinson (ed.), *Sovereign Subjects – Indigenous Sovereignty Matters* (2007)
- Vandana Shiva, *Globalization's New Wars – Seed, Water and Life forms* (2005)
- Arundhati Roy, *The Cost of Living* (1999) and *Power Politics* (2002)
- Barry Barclay, *Mana Tuturu: Maori Treasures and International Property Rights* (2005)
- Helen Tiffin and Graham Huggan, *Postcolonial Ecocriticism* (2009)
- Gayatri Chakravorty Spivak, *Other Asias* (2007)

Postcolonial literature and the canon, postcolonial canons (some critical works)

- Robert Fraser, *Book History Through Postcolonial Eyes: Rewriting The Script* (2008)
- John Thieme, *Postcolonial Contexts – Writing Back to the Canon* (2001)
- Aijaz Ahmad, *In Theory: Classes, Nations, Literatures* (1999)
- Gayatri Spivak, *In Other Worlds: Essays in Cultural Politics* (1987)
- Graham Huggan, *The Postcolonial Exotic-Marketing the Margins* (2001)
- Roy Miki and Smaro Kamboureli, *Trans.Can.Lit: Resituating the Study of Canadian Literature* (2007)
- Mary Hammond and Robert Fraser, *Books without Borders, Vol. 1: The Cross National Dimension in Print Culture* (2008)

RESEARCH

- Compare and contrast different accounts of the term 'postcolonial' you have found in your reading and research in this subject area? What do they have in common? How do they differ in their definition of the horizons of the term?
- Look at the syllabus of the module (in postcolonial literatures) you are studying. What questions would you ask about it if you were focusing on it as a 'canon'? What areas are represented?

What not? Discuss the factors that might have shaped selection and organization.

- Identify three reasons why diasporas are an important site of discussion in postcolonial literatures. Make a list of keywords or terms associated with diasporas and their study. Research two of these keywords in more detail.

Extended research topic

- Pick a country or a continent as your topic of study. Consider some of the following tasks, topics and questions:
- What are the key moments of diaspora in the history of your chosen location?
- How do their diasporas differ across time? Do the different generations of migrants move to the same locations? What other diasporas might they build ties with or alternately find themselves in conflict with? How does the experience of diasporas differ across generations? How are experiences inflected by race, language, class, gender?
- Make a list of some writers or artists from your chosen location exploring diasporic identities (music, art, drama, poetry, film, life writing as well as fiction and short stories).
- Identify some theorists of diaspora – compare and contrast the work of two theorists.
- Explore the representation of diasporas and diasporic identities in two theorists and/or writers/artists.
- Explore the relationship between the form of the writing/artwork and what it says about diasporic identities.

PART TWO

TEXTS

CHAPTER THREE

READINGS OF KEY TEXTS

CHIMAMANDA NGOZI ADICHIE, *PURPLE HIBISCUS* (2004)

Adichie's first novel narrates the coming of age of a young Nigerian girl of Igbo descent, Kambili Achike, against the background of an oppressive political regime that reflects the general turmoil of post-colonial Nigeria. With successive periods of restrictive military rule since its Independence in 1960 and a bloody civil war (1967–70) after the secession of the short-lived Republic of Biafra, Nigeria's political history has been extraordinarily fraught. Consequently, *Purple Hibiscus* explores the social ramifications of this continuing climate of political unease, in which the legacies of Nigeria's colonial histories still knot its landscapes and where economic inequalities are exacerbated by the unequal distribution of the nation's oil wealth, fuelling ethnic and religious tension and militancy. Such legacies distort the promises of postcolonial nationhood and threaten their more various and productive expressions.

Kambili's growth is complicated by the position of her father, Eugene. He is a prominent figure in the public sphere as the owner of a newspaper critical of the government and its leader, 'Big Oga'. This oppositional stance generates a set of pressures that place the family under distinct forms of stress and insecurity. The incidents Kambili narrates in the opening section of the novel, 'Breaking Gods – Palm Sunday', represent her attempt to define when 'things started to fall apart at home' (1). The moment of fracture she chooses details an instance of familial insurrection when her brother Jaja defies their father's authority, thus challenging his privileging of Catholic doctrine and his rejection of the spiritual beliefs of his own Igbo culture.

Attempting to locate a distinct point of fracture illustrates the difficulty of easily distinguishing the clew of family. As Kambili quickly concedes, if Jaja's defiance marks one kind of breach, its origins lie in earlier events, in journeys from their home town, Enuga, to their parents' home in Abba, the dwelling place of their grandfather Papa-Nnukwu, and to neighbouring Nsukka and the university campus home of their Aunty Ifeoma. In both, they observe a more inquisitive approach to Catholic doctrine and a more positive account of Igbo values and traditions: 'Nsukka started it all . . . Nsukka began to lift the silence' (16).

Kambili's review of the time prior to this breach, those 'years when Jaja and Mama and I spoke more with our spirits than with our lips' (16) constitutes the main body of the novel, 'Speaking with Our Spirits – Before Palm Sunday'. The traumatic effects of this period are then made apparent in 'The Pieces of Gods – After Palm Sunday' where Jaja's defiance, at once 'too new, too foreign' (258) for a nervous Kambili, slowly translates into more enabling forms of self-assertion and belief. This is punctured by the turn their mother's fearful and brutal experience at the hands of Eugene takes, resulting in her slow poisoning of him. The concluding section, 'A Different Silence – The Present', explores the outcome of Jaja's decision to take responsibility for Eugene's death and details how his imprisonment reshapes internal family relations in the aftermath.

While in this shuttling between past, present and future, the novel eschews the linear trajectory of the conventional *bildungsroman*, its primary concern remains the coming to consciousness of Kambili and her changing relationships with family, community and nation. It traces her fledgling efforts to define herself in a variety of surroundings (school and church) and to imagine a viable independent future, to translate silence into speech, and painful suppression into self-expression in a climate of stultifying domestic restriction that comes to mirror the extremes of the public realm. In this, Adichie's focus on 'Palm Sunday' as a tipping point, is not just a way of marking time or structuring action, but of making visible wider structures, orders, coherences that cross the private as the public realm, that owe as much to the past as the present, and of drawing attention to the realities that belie surface appearances and order.

The politics of 'Palm Sunday' – colonialism, capitalism and Christianity

In Christian and Catholic tradition, 'Palm Sunday' is a day of celebration and the offering of palms is a sign of hospitality and honour. The story Kambili remembers however, is less about honour than it is about the traumatic confusion of honour and dishonour, resulting in the violent eruption of her father, Eugene. Kambili's memory of this day initiates a series of painful recognitions. 'Palm Sunday' names the defining role punitive interpretations of Catholic doctrine will play in the lives of the novel's protagonists, but the 'Palm' in 'Palm Sunday' also registers Nigeria's colonial histories and how Christianity is tied to a wider set of economic, social and environmental interventions with long lasting legacies. It summons the long history of trade between Europe and West Africa in the African oil palm and its products, which dates back to the 1480s and was at least as important for the industrial development that fuelled colonial expansion in the nineteenth century as the contemporary trade in petroleum (oil) (Wenzel 2006). Palm is thus mnemonic of those local and transnational circuits of power transformed by the passage of European colonialisms in West Africa, for as Jennifer Wenzel has noted, 'Nigeria's Oil Rivers region was named for palm oil, not petroleum' (452) and its contemporary petroleum economy has 'literally been super imposed over (or excavated under) the palm belt of the Niger Delta' (453). 'Palm Sunday' thus conjoins the economic interest of the colonial powers in Nigeria and the ideological work of Christianity in securing and maintaining Western dominance and it invites us to consider the continuing and changing relationship between colonial and postcolonial systems of production and exchange.

In resurrecting too a resonant image of precolonial indigenous social life and its diffuse economies, palm is affiliated in *Purple Hibiscus* with Igbo history and the cultural traditions associated with Kambili's grandfather, Papa-Nnwuku and her aunt, Ifeoma. So, when, for example, Kambili's cousins, Amaka and Obiora, disagree about whether they should continue to 'bleach' palm oil to render it functional for cooking, rather than spending valuable resources on the vegetable oil that is more costly to procure, their disagreements highlight conflicting attitudes to the question of how best to advance the cause of cultural conservation and national renewal. In light of the unstable political climate and the lack of opportunities for Ifeoma's advancement, Obiora is keen to leave Nigeria and doesn't share what he considers to be Amaka's unrealistic desire to stay and 'fix' the country, borne out of her anger at the disenfranchisement of ordinary citizens. 'Why', she asks, 'do we have to run away from our own country? Why can't we fix it?'(232). Amaka is fearful of the cultural losses that flight might engender. 'How will I get Fela tapes in America, eh?' (277), she asks Kambili, articulating a newly fragile sense of her bonds to culture, in the aftermath of the death of her beloved Papa-Nnwuku, explaining too her insistence on continuing to 'bleach' the palm oil as if to stave off the certainty of the family's impending flight from Nigeria.

Here the ritual of bleaching the oil seems to illustrate the necessity of continuing to 'process' tradition in order to access its dynamic nurturing properties. However, the term 'bleaching' also introduces a more ambivalent edge to Adichie's account of the importance of Igbo traditions to Amaka's sense of self. This ambivalence derives from how the term invokes the racially charged social practice of skin-bleaching among some African and Afro-Caribbean communities. This is one expression of the violations of black subjectivity generated by the pigmentocratic nature of colonial constructions of race in which the historic privileging of whiteness violently disrupts what Frantz Fanon terms in *Black Skin, White Masks* the 'bodily schema' of the black subject. As Fanon explains, the visceral experience of colonial racism can skewer the formation of black identity such that it can produce 'blackness' as a kind of 'corporeal malediction' (Fanon 1986: 111) and install as a consequence, a damaging desire for whiteness, a wishing to be white. In this context, skin-bleaching, expressive of a distinct set of fears and desires, might be understood as propelled by the ambivalence generated by violations of black identity formation, activating fantasies of racial dissolution or dilution. Adichie's use of the term, 'bleaching', to talk about culture rather than race carries this ambivalence over from one arena to the other, suggesting perhaps that what Amaka may be accessing is an already 'deracinated' form of culture, one distorted or diluted in its passage through colonialism. This may reflect the changing fortunes of the palm economy, itself displaced by the rise of the contemporary petroleum economy. As Jennifer Wenzel observes, 'palm oil production and exports decreased after the 1950s' and 'Nigeria became a net importer of vegetable oil in the 1980s' (453). This change amplifies Nigeria's uncertain position in global systems of exchange as the privileging of petroleum production (accounting for over 90% of exports) and its adverse environmental effects increase dependency on foreign imports for basic food security. This is a challenge Nigeria shares with other globalized economies but here it emphasizes the dangers posed by the imbalances that attend new forms of resource extraction, as locations that were rich in more various and environmentally sustainable locally produced resources gradually become more dependent on a single, unstable, non-renewable 'cash crop' (oil). Thus, the vegetable oil that Obiora prefers as an alternative to palm oil represents the nexus of challenges posed by Nigeria's participation in and penetration by global economic systems shaped by colonialism, but also too by the cultural distortions that attend its prominence.

The identification of palm oil and palm-wine with indigenous cultural traditions is longstanding in Nigerian literature in English, stretching back to Amos Tutuola's *The Palm-Wine Drinkard* (1952) and is reiterated severally in Adichie's novel, notably in Kambili's choking on the smoke produced by burning the oil: 'It was clear that I was unused to bleaching palm oil, that I was used to vegetable oil, which did not need bleaching' (264). Here, Kambili's choking fit signals her unfamiliarity with Igbo culture compared to Amaka, a budding symbol of a confident and inquiring Afrocentrism. For Amaka, Kambili's ignorance of Igbo culture is initially diagnosed as an arrogant expression of cultural disinterest cushioned by the surface accoutrements of affluence (satellite television, the latest stereo) that she initially perceives as abundantly available to Kambili. Kambili can't voice the truth, that such distance is a product of her father's excessive fears of the dangers posed by internal and external cultural influences: 'I wanted to tell her that although huge satellite dishes lounged on top of the houses in Enugu and here [Abba], we did not watch TV. Papa did not pencil in TV time on our schedules' (79). When Amaka comes to realize that Kambili's reticence is a product not of disinterest but of Eugene's controlling behaviour, she becomes an important source of social and cultural transmission. She introduces Kambili to the music of Fela, teaches her to prepare foodstuffs and entrusts a precious picture of Papa-Nnwuku to her care. Yet, even as Amaka's recognitions come to signal her more nuanced understanding of Kambili's position, Adichie's novel still hovers uncertainly around the assertion that affluence breeds damaging forms of cultural alienation while economic privation produces cultural resourcefulness. The scar, 'shaped like a dagger', that Kambili notices on the neck of her father's intermediary and chaperone, Kevin, is the result of 'a fall from a palm tree in his hometown in the Niger Delta area, a few years ago while on vacation' (63). Like the choking smoke it is a gruesome symbol of the physical perils that greet those divorced from or forgetful of the potency or fertility of local traditions. Of course this assertion is also complicated by Adichie's critical portrait of Eugene's religious values and how they condition his management of both his economic resources and his attitudes to Igbo culture.

Palm memorializes too how indigenous cultures are transformed by colonialism yet survive and flourish to transform in turn the culture of the colonizer as it puts down roots in African locations. In this respect, Adichie's attention is focused on a distinct set of tensions and continuities; between the forms of Catholic doctrine privileged by Christian missionaries in Nigeria and the indigenous practices they initially sought to displace or harness. Eugene's dismissal of Papa-Nnwuku's spiritual beliefs as 'heathen' combined with his privileging of English over Igbo articulate the monstrous elements of colonialism's ravaging of the culture of the colonized, its tendency to disavow and diminish indigenous cultures and belief systems and to install and promote the culture of the colonizer as *the* site of civilization and value. Eugene is figurative of the dangers to one's sense of self of internalizing the values of the colonizer and of becoming in the process, as Ifeoma has it, 'too much of a colonial product' (13). Here colonialism is disease and Eugene's increasingly violent rejection of his Igbo father, its pathology. Kambili remembers how Ifeoma observes Eugene's reverential attitude to the English language in 'a mild, forgiving way, as if it were not Papa's fault, as one would talk about a person who were shouting gibberish from a severe case of malaria' (13). Malaria, infiltrating the body and the mind, is a potent metaphor through which to explore both the physical and psychological ills of colonialism and it is one that has a distinct lineage in colonial and postcolonial literatures. The Caribbean poet, Derek Walcott, has spoken of such damage as a kind of 'malarial enervation' in describing the forms of cultural inferiority that attend the sway of colonial ideologies in the lives of the colonized (1998: 4). In *Purple Hibiscus*, the violence deployed by Eugene in the mistaken belief that it will secure adherence to his beliefs is a powerful expression of the psychological damage accrued in his conversion, the extreme elements of which reiterate early missionary attitudes. Such violence, as Adichie reminds us in her figuration of Eugene, continues to be transmitted across the generations, crossing public and private realms. The damage to the body politic in postcolonial Nigeria mapped in Adichie's attention to state corruption, censorship and torture is mirrored in Eugene's tyrannical approach to family and both are tied in part to the forms of damage inculcated in colonial encounter. Adichie makes particular and repeated use of the physical body as an index of wider social ills and traumatic effects. In Eugene's bloated body and engorged face, Jaja's mangled finger, Mama's bruises and miscarriages, Kambili's disembodiment, Adichie offers bodily damage as a resonant archive of the violent legacies of earlier colonial and more recent postcolonial histories of cultural fragmentation and alienation. In deploying such powerful images of bodily suffering to emphasize the real effects of power on bodies (directly and indirectly) Adichie may also reinforce rather than challenge common equations of bodily impairment with other forms of injury; emphasizing powerlessness at the expense of recognizing ongoing forms of agency. The greater focus in Adichie's novel on Kambili's gradual empowerment and embodiment works to dissolve some of these tendencies.

In exploring how Christianity might be renewed by a more inclusive attitude to indigenous and animist belief systems, Adichie develops Chinua Achebe's formative attention to the decimations of Igbo culture wrought by the politics of colonial encounter in Nigeria in *Things Fall Apart* (1958). This intention to revisit Achebe is signalled in multiple ways. The opening line of *Purple Hibiscus*, repeating the title of Achebe's novel, immediately opens a dialogue with his concerns. If Achebe emphasizes the *conflict* between differing belief systems in the moment of contact in *Things Fall Apart*, Adichie's attention to the later development of Christianity in Nigeria suggests that Achebe's initial focus on conflict might overlook the continuing forms of *connection* between imported and indigenous systems. Her delineation of the hybridizing of Western religious traditions in African locations articulates the need to address and understand the continuing mutual fertilization of traditions, as much as it seeks to revisit the dynamics of contact. If Eugene represents one tradition, Ifeoma represents another; one well versed in distinguishing the pitfalls as well as the values of embracing Western and Igbo culture and negotiating the spaces between them. Ifeoma refuses Papa-Nnwuku's assertion that it is missionary education per se that is to blame for

Eugene's rejection of Igbo culture. She argues that her own experiences of a missionary education produced different outcomes. Ifeoma represents the development of an inclusive set of beliefs and values empowered not endangered by its encounters with other cultures. However, the narration of Ifeoma's eventual flight from Nigeria, with the evisceration of the university by the governing regime, illustrates the fragility of such visions and the dangers posed by their collapse; the hardening of religious and ethnic rivalries and traditions.

Gender in Africa

Such visions of inclusivity are tempered by both Ifeoma's and Amaka's differently accented awareness of a challenging set of contiguities between Igbo culture and Catholicism, rooted in a shared patriarchal bias and exhibited in their tendency to devalue and disempower women. This bias in Igbo culture is apparent when Papa-Nnwuku dismisses the importance of Ifeoma's assertion of her ideological difference from Eugene: 'But you are a woman. You do not count' (83). Nnwuku's subsequent explanation of this point reveals that a key site of traction in his disagreement with Eugene is Christianity's levelling of the hierarchical relationships between father and son in Igbo culture which he sees as directly responsible for Eugene's poor treatment of him. Eugene lists other Igbo hierarchies as a key source of his own conflicts with his father's culture. After a visit to the local Igwe, greeted by Beatrice in 'the traditional way that women were supposed to, bending low and offering him her back so that he would pat it with his fan made of the soft, straw-coloured tail of an animal' (93), Eugene's furious response focuses on his sense that the social practice of bowing to another human being is 'ungodly', a sinful obeisance incompatible with his faith. What neither Eugene nor his father choose to recognize is the fact that the values of both Igbo culture and the Catholic faith are stretched, like the Igwe's fan, across the bodies of women. Equally, Papa-Nnwuku's explanation of the underlying rules of the 'mmuo' ceremony delineate the sanctions that accompany women's roles in Igbo culture just as the dissection of Catholic orthodoxy illustrates the heightened concerns both cultures share in the anxious surveillance of women's bodies and behaviours.

Ifeoma and Amaka differently represent the difficult task facing African women in combating the restrictive ideologies and values embedded in both. While Ifeoma often stands for pragmatic compromise, Amaka's battles reiterate her challenge of base principles. Ifeoma strategically manipulates Igbo social ties and obligations in order to contest Eugene's treatment of Kambili, Jaja and their mother and she illustrates how tradition might be transformed in order to shore up communal ties and facilitate female empowerment. Amaka challenges the limits of the Church's adaptation to its African locations and the forms of compromise that both her mother and Father Amadi have made with its defining tenets. Her refusal to observe those practices that continue to devalue Igbo culture, like the taking of an English confirmation name, is an indictment of the Church's extant failures to cherish women and Igbo culture equally. Amaka represents too a generation whose creative energies are often rerouted elsewhere, in the coil of diaspora. In *Purple Hibiscus* the family's departure for America leaves us with an ambiguous glimpse of the challenges facing African cultures on the ground once talent is forced to migrate, but those recreations (of self, home, place) re/produced in diaspora are the focus of Adichie's recent collection of short stories, *The Thing Around Your Neck* (2009).

This rerouting is apparent too in the frustration of Jaja's early hopes and dreams. The nurturing climate of Ifeoma's Nsukka is embodied in the novel's titular image of hope and fertility, the purple hibiscus that Ifeoma gifts to Jaja, 'rare, fragrant with the undertones of freedom' (16). But the thwarting of Jaja's raised ambitions in his assuming of responsibility for his mother's poisoning of his father, reiterates the costs exacted by the failure to break with the more stultifying elements of tradition. Kambili observes how the traumatic and isolating effects of taking responsibility for his mother's crime translate in the aftermath. He shows signs of repeating rather than breaking with the damaging past. Visiting Jaja in prison, Kambili is startled both by his sudden insinuation that their mother's head is improperly covered and the abject nature of her mother's response to this rebuke: 'I stare in amazement. Jaja has never noticed what anybody wears. Mama hastily unties and reties her scarf – and this time, she knots it twice and tight at the back of her head' (306). Already injured by her life-experiences, Kambili observes her mother's slow unravelling, her inability to find a place in the world in which her self-definition is not wholly shaped by her relations with the men in it, first Eugene, now Jaja: '[H]er limp has become more noticeable, her body moving sideways with each step' (306). Reiterating a tendency to collapse physical impairment and loss, Adichie hints here at the continuing forms of subjection created by the convergence of conservative religious and cultural values which delimit women's self-possession and individuality.

Learning to laugh

Laughter in *Purple Hibiscus* is an expression of social ease, joy, inclusivity and community. Historically associated with traditions of carnival and their legislated inversions of dominant orders and powers (Bakhtin 1984, Stallybrass and White 1986), laughter is disruptive. It cuts through restraint and is a powerful antidote to the forms of silencing Kambili and her mother experience. Adichie's novel continually juxtaposes the life-giving quality of laughter with the morbid character of silence. Song is the means through which Kambili relearns self-expression, facilitated by her immersion in Nsukka and her observation of the confidence, curiosity and independence that Ifeoma cultivates in her children: 'Laughter always rang out in Aunty Ifeoma's house . . . it bounced around all the walls, all the rooms' (140). Laughter is allied with the family's joyous appreciation of Igbo song, a feature shared with Father Amadi who develops a friendship with Kambili. Kambili's learning to laugh is an index of her coming to self-possession and embodiment, a glimpse, however brief, of an alternative world to the one her father imagines for her. The seditious nature of this imagining is indicated by its association in dreams with a feeling of possession by the laughter of others (88). Slowly this ghostly feeling of possession by others is relieved by self-possession and it signals the reclamation of the body previously constricted by violence and fear. The loosening character of song is conjoined with the spontaneous character of laughter as vivid sources of cultural reclamation and nourishment. In the novel's closing sequence, laughter and song constitute an important reminder for Kambili of the possibilities once unleashed by Nsukka: 'I laughed loudly, above Fela's stringent singing . . . [b]ecause Nsukka could free something deep inside your belly that would rise up to your throat and come out as a freedom song. As laughter' (299).

Nsukka forms the connective tissue between *Purple Hibiscus* and Adichie's *Half of a Yellow Sun* (2006), which turns away from the image of a degraded Nsukka that preoccupies Kambili when she visits it after Ifeoma and her cousins have departed for America. Then, the campus reflects the abandonment that has overtaken those who remain behind, but its glistening in a 'searing sun' (298) that can 'suck the moisture from the bone marrow' (298) is, as Lily Mabura notes, a luminous revenant of an earlier time when Nsukka was once prominent in the nascent Republic of Biafra, whose creation and brief life is the subject of the later novel tracking as it does the divergent fates of two sisters across its troubling divides.

PATRICIA GRACE, *DOGSIDE STORY* (2001)

The Māori 'Renaissance'

Patricia Grace, Hone Tuwhare and Witi Ihimaera are the writers most often associated with the 'Māori Renaissance', a term often used to describe the resurgence in indigenous cultural expression and production from the 1970s onwards, informed by the galvanizing influence of a range of indigenous political and cultural movements aimed at reversing the depredations of land rights, language and culture. Contesting the adverse influences of colonization and the assimilative strategies of a hegemonic Pākehā (European) culture, the movements that defined the 'Renaissance' demanded a greater recognition of biculturalism as a defining tenet of the nation. Biculturalism refers to the greater recognition afforded the unique claims of Māori as indigenous peoples with substantive historic relationships to Aotearoa/New Zealand and with Pākehā culture, even as the terms under which state sponsored policies of biculturalism promote Māori culture are the subject of continuing debate. This specific claim to and recognition of place inheres in their position as signatories of Te Tiriti o Waitanga/the Treaty of Waitangi (1840). The Treaty assigns certain inalienable rights to indigenous people, although for a long period these rights were ignored by the colonizing culture. The Waitangi Tribunal, established in 1975, under the Treaty of Waitangi Act, exists to address the breaches in promises made to Māori under the terms of the Treaty, a factor that has had important constitutional implications that have in no small measure also shaped official policies of biculturalism since the Act's passing. Waitangi has long been seen as 'founding' document of the nation. It is a key site through which discourses of nation are reshaped and it remains an ongoing site of contest, subject to disparate indigenous claims regarding the security of land, foreshore, coast and culture rights. Notwithstanding, it establishes and anchors Māori claims to distinct forms of internal sovereignty. Multiculturalism, by contrast, in seeking to recognize the diverse claims of a range of cultures and to reflect the changing demographic structure of New Zealand, situates Māori *as one of many* groups with distinctive claims. It is thus often seen as a threat to the hard-won recognitions afforded by biculturalism, for the advance of multiculturalism as a state approved discourse is one that is often seen to obscure Māori place, suggesting for many critics something of how the state continues to manage and thus dilute certain forms of 'rights' recognition to its own ends.

Historically, the 'Renaissance' has been understood as the continuation of older expressions of Māori nationalism from the mid-nineteenth century onwards (Williams 1997, 2006). One of its more distinctive features is the emergence of a generation of indigenous writers newly engaged with imported European literary forms in articulating the particularities of Māori cultures and values to diverse audiences. I emphasize the plurality rather than the singularity of cultures and values here for although the term 'Māori' commonly refers to the indigenous people of Aotearoa/New Zealand as a whole, its usage as such can also eclipse the heterogeneity of differences, of tribe (iwi) and tribal affiliation within and between Māori. Writers like Grace and Ihimaera often interrogate and rework the models engaged, indigenizing or estranging those forms in distinctive ways, precisely in order to make them speak to a variety of local contexts and audiences. In the process, new forms are created in the sites of exchange between writers and between indigenous and imported cultural traditions.

Ihimaera and Grace have been at the forefront of debates about survival, cultural resistance and renewal for decades. Sometimes, their early work has been seen as nostalgic in its address of rural communities under threat (Keown 2005:149) or as marked by a tendency to construe the indigene as victim of colonial intransigence, a concern voiced by Alan Duff, author of *Once Were Warriors* (1990). With regard to the latter charge, it could be argued that Duff underestimates the sophistication and nuance in both writers' critique as well as celebration of Māori culture and politics. For example, Grace is much more interested in debates *between* Māori and other Oceanic or Pacific Rim cultures than she is in reading that history and culture through a singular set of conflicts – Māori versus Pākehā. While the dynamics of colonial encounter and their effects are a clear basis of concern she is also very clearly preoccupied with connections and divisions *within* and *without* indigenous cultures. If many critics read such reworkings of received models as a counter colonizing strategy, what such strategies might achieve or what costs might be incurred by indigenous writers in mobilizing such strategies are themselves partly the subject of Ihimaera's current retrospective dialogue with his own early creative work. Committed to rewriting five of his already published novels and collections of short stories, Ihimaera's undertaking has not been without controversy, partly because it is both a relatively unusual and hugely interesting creative and political move. Ihimaera explains the enterprise as a product of a longer process of self-reflection as well as ambivalence about the legacies of his engagements with an imported culture and its literary traditions (Ihimaera and Mares 2009). In doing so he amplifies the distorting effects of the historical, social and political imperatives of the early 1970s on his work, citing the earlier work's sometimes reliance on stereotype or of a view of indigenous culture as on the wane as exemplary of the pressures imposed by the imperatives of the earlier period. It is a move that reflects too his own sense of what constitutes his responsibility to culture and it emphasizes the specific *kaupapa* (purpose) of literature as a dynamic, mobile repository of indigenous cultural identity and history – as a living, mutable, communal script or *korero* (discussion). This emphasis on the mobility of indigenous culture finds distinct expression too in Patricia Grace's recent novel, *Dogside Story*.

Dogside Story

This novel addresses the question of intergenerational conflict and change in indigenous communities. It concerns the experiences of a young man, Rua, and his relationship with his daughter, Kiri/Kid. Grace traces Rua's assumption of his previously unacknowledged paternal responsibilities for Kid. In this, he has to acknowledge too that Kid is the result of incest, of relations between Rua and his half-sister, Ani Wainoa. Here, Grace excavates how his coming to bear responsibility is inseparable from, indeed, is actively informed by the growth of the *whānau* (extended family) and the reconsideration of its collective responsibilities. For Rua's intervention in Kid's care upsets existing arrangements (that have contributed to her neglect), generating conflict between three generations, the elders (Wai, Arch, Tini and Pop Henry), the 'The Two Aunts', Amiria and Babs, entrusted with Kid's care, and Rua, Jase and Bones, the young adults of the group. This crisis unfolds against the background destruction of the community's *wharekai* (eating house) and its necessary reconstruction as the life space of the *whānau*. Millennium celebrations become the focus of communal efforts to raise funds for the wharekai's reconstruction which in turn generate questions for the community about how they manage and consolidate their own material and cultural resources. Part of Rua's coming to consciousness is his facing up to past ghosts, particularly the car accident which robs him of two of his cousins and his leg. Rua's lost limb and his responses to it mirror the challenges facing 'Dogside' as it seeks to address the questions posed by Rua's intervention in Kid's care. Indeed, Clare Barker suggests that Rua's 'micro' experience of embodied difference is instrumental in (re) generating 'models' of care that address 'how "health" might be configured on the macro levels of family and community'. She argues further that the disability narrative mobilized both 'anticipates and informs (as well as it reflects) approaches to community and *cultural* healing . . . [that] ultimately intersect with the principles of indigenous sovereignty that inform Grace's writing' (2008: 123).

Those principles are reiterated in the communal resolutions found to the crisis, particularly in the insurgent act of storytelling that accompanies the eventual confrontation of Amiria and Babs at the *hui* (gathering) called to resolve the crisis. This shared storytelling is also a communal act of truth-telling, a coming together 'to bear witness' (282) to a testimony that speaks of an older tragedy buried in the divisive effects of historic dispossessions and alienation from land. The Aunts reveal the existence of a secret will, which they fear means they can be dispossessed of their home if existing arrangements for Kid dissolve. On hearing this, Tini reasserts the importance of the ties that continue to bind the lives of the people and of those traditions that preceded the 'land-grab' buried in the Treaty of Waitangi (1840), despite its promises of recognition and inalienable rights. Its damaging legacies and divisions live on in the will that is the source of the Aunts' terror, against which Tini asserts an older sovereignty than that claimed by *Pākehā* (European) law, here deemed a mere interruption of indigenous traditions. She reaffirms the sisters' place in the community not on the basis of an imported law, but an indigenous one: 'We are your witnesses, and we know your land, your land with not one broken tree' (290). Securing Amiria's agreement to dispense with the corroding document and enfolding the Aunts' into the capacious law of the *whānau*, Tini creates the space for Rua's plans to build a future with Kid to flourish.

Creation stories – two women and a canoe

Dogside Story opens with a creation story that is also *whakapapa* (genealogy). It offers a playful account of the origins of North and South Island Māori identities, imaginatively rendered in the delineation of longstanding divisions between two communities, 'Godside' and 'Dogside', originating in a conflict between two sisters, Ngarua and Maranenohonoho, over the ownership of their dead brother's canoe. This story is an important thematic precursor or frame to the analysis of history and culture that Grace offers. She anticipates and deflects a range of assumptions that commonly attend representations of indigenous cultures and histories from outside indigenous locations. Grace's creation story gestures to histories *aside* from those which situate indigenous identities as beginning with and determined by colonial history and experience. She also destabilizes those Eurocentric visions that consign Māori culture to the role of colourful backdrop to European action, or are preoccupied with the history of the 'contact zone', 'those social spaces, where disparate cultures meet, clash, and grapple with each other, often in highly asymmetrical relations of domination and subordination – like colonialism, slavery or their aftermaths' (Pratt 1992: 4). Grace's *whakapapa* reaches farther back and focuses instead on the microhistory of the Pacific and its diasporas, on those journeyings that result in Polynesian settlement of New Zealand between the eighth and thirteenth century; a focus that asserts also the ancestry of the Māori as 'first' comers or first settlers. Her emphasis in the creation story is on the developing character of each community and the misconceptions that arise out of the formative divisions between them. Her 'dogside story' settles, for example, upon how dogsiders understanding of themselves as the 'inlet crossers', as 'movers, changers, seekers' (2001:11) becomes a defining feature of their identity.

Grace examines how stories about this 'original' crossing are generated and sustained *within* culture and represented in the official 'History' or 'creation story' of Aotearea/New Zealand. This story is expanded and revised at several junctures and it is thus not unlike the *tahuhu*, 'the backbone of the ancestor' (268), that is regularly resituated as her 'Dogside' community moves from old to new *wharenui* (meeting house). The question of cultural transmission was clearly a defining political concern of the 'Renaissance' and as the passage of the creation story indicates, it remains a key site in Grace's account of intergenerational change and conflict within Māori communities. Its function is primarily to provide a set of contexts for the story that follows about the navigation of social divisions within culture. In narrating these divisions, Grace also offers a wider examination of the mobility of Māori culture, its capacities for change strengthened by its ongoing hybridization and adaptation, an attention to which productively complicates longer standing conceptions of indigeneity as a sign of rootedness and/or mooring in place.

The *whakapapa* delineated is also about an approach to culture that Grace sees as distinctively Māori and perhaps also distinctively postcolonial in its political thrust; improvisation. It is about improvised beginnings, settlements formed by accident and on impulse rather than intention, in a stubborn squabble between two grieving sisters over a canoe which ends up at the bottom of the sea anyway. It is about the minor rather than the epic, smaller local crossings rather than the larger transnational journeyings of Captain James Cook or Louis-Antoine de Bougainville that litter dominant accounts of European beginnings in Australia and New Zealand. However, in focusing on how such accidents are turned into a demonstration of principled intent, are *made* across time into narratives of difference, Grace is, in parodic fashion, addressing the artificiality of 'History' as founding fiction, excavating how communities and nations actively *produce* their histories and myths out of what are, perhaps, less than epic stories. They become epic in the retelling, in the translation and cultivation of beginnings *as* origin.

A focus on improvised beginnings, which deviate from familiar scriptings of origin, alert us to the ways in which identities are performances, and suggest that indigeneity too, as the matrix of rights, belongings, histories, laws that configure indigenous identities, needs to be understood as a distinct kind of performance of relationship to place, memory, culture, locations. For Grace, improvisation is central to the survival of the *whānau* and a critical tool in challenging relations of power. It has a particular purchase and political purpose in a site where the strained relations between biculturalism and multiculturalism could be seen to facilitate the advance of a 'compulsory nationalism' that upholds the maintenance of a homogenizing set of (national) scripts, that tends to support the (economic) interests of non-Māori 'second comers' at some cost to Māori interests (Turner 2008: 9). The improvisation that accompanies parody can be understood as part of a larger armoury which makes visible the operations of power and the values and ideologies on which it is premised. Like Grace, the Canadian writer of Cherokee-Greek descent, Thomas King, illustrates the flexibility of parody and its long tenured history as a political strategy in indigenous cultural performance, in his *A Short History of Indians in Canada* (2005) and *One Good Story, That One* (1993). Both of these collections of short stories, like Grace's *Dogside Story* and Alexis Wright's epic tale of the Gulf coast peoples of Queensland, *Carpentaria* (2006), are fuelled by the recognition of the wider cultural impetus of story in histories of indigenous and non-indigenous self-definition.

The cultural precedence of story is reflected in individual terms in Kid's direct address of Rua. The first words we hear her speak to him apart from his name, are the words, 'Tell me', 'Tell me Rua', an invocation that we latterly come to understand as a plea for a different scripting of her 'origins', an alternative creation story to that offered by her negligent aunties, Amiria and Babs, who insist that she was 'cracked out of an egg' or as she has it, 'a seagull shitted me' (126). Buried inside the precursory creation story then and its parodic address of how we make our history out of story, is an acknowledgement of the formative structuring of self, individual and communal that creation stories as archives of culture offer. In exposing 'History' as a 'Story' and in analysing the subsequent 'storying' of 'History', Grace's work is both metafictional and metahistorical. It illustrates the mutual embedding of fiction and history and confirms the role of fiction as an alternative (historical) archive.

What might be at stake in revisiting and resituating beginnings (creation stories) is amply illustrated in Grace's account of the ways in which 'The Crossing' is interpreted in a variety of mediums across generations; in its continuing and changing role as a versatile cultural resource. Grace's account of the mural which newly adorns the community's *wharenui* suggests some of the questions that such

transformations might raise, including those which attend its translation from one medium to another, from say, an oral to a visual one.
The mural is produced by young artists 'on a Maccess scheme' (141)
reiterating how the reproduction of Māori culture is embedded in
and often attendant upon a wider economy or hierarchy of interests
which in turn may shape its appearances and/or reception. It renders
the creation story in epic terms, exaggerating the warrior like status
of Ngarua as an icon of *Māoritanga* (Māoriness), 'standing large in
a great carved war canoe, prow feathers and all' (141). At the same
time, it diminishes the status of her sister, Maraenohonoho, 'on the
back of a knock-kneed horse wielding, not a lump of driftwood but
something resembling a jousting lance' (141). Dogsiders' mural,
Grace implies, thus transforms and exaggerates formative divisions.
Its iconography accentuates Dogsiders as the natural inheritors of an
'authentic' Māoriness, thus associating 'Godsiders' in turn with
deculturation, with cultural dilution. Here both Maraenohonoho's
horse and jousting lance might suggest her alignment with the adverse
incursions of a later (Anglo) colonizing culture. Grace's account
of the transformation of Maraenohonoho illustrates some of the
ways in which a Māori historiography might assimilate and actively
transform diverse experiences of colonial history; how colonial
history might, in a corrosive manner, lend itself to the amplification
of pre-existing divisions or alternately provide a site for their displacement, or indeed their intermeshing. She also echoes the fears
voiced by Alan Duff about the dangers of accentuating versions of
Māori identity centred on notions of warriorhood divorced from the
values and contexts that historically informed them, as explored in
his novel, *Once Were Warriors*. The general thrust of her vision however, in its portrait of a dynamic, inclusive, holistic and adaptive
Māori community stands in some contrast to his bleaker account of
a marginalized, destructive and degraded one.

The mural generates a dialogue within the community about
representation, interpretation and evaluation, about how best to
preserve and transmit the past: 'Some like the mural. Others think it
is modern and hideous and say that ancestress Ngarua had been
made to look like a gang member or a bikie. They're awaiting an
opportunity to paint it over' (141). Here, Grace raises critical questions
about the ownership of culture, its malleability and mobility. Culture
is shaped by the life of the community but the community is not isolated from the world but an active part of it. The 'contemporary

marae' or 'te turangawaewae o te iwi' (the standing place of the people) is thus a key site of negotiation and debate where the individual and the community both 'negotiate the potential and situational forms and meanings of contemporary Māori identity through various modes of cultural performance' (Allen 2002:10) that includes different forms of story. Indeed, the role of *whakapapa* as a positive source of unity and law over the divisions (imposed by Waitangi) is reasserted by Grace in the final section of the novel as the community face the revelations generated in the space of the *hui*. There, the elders reach for the story of Ngarua and Maraenohonoho as legal precedent and moral lesson, as an example of the importance of dissolving past jealousies, of dispensing with the source of pain and division precisely in order to live otherwise. Here Ngarua's initial decision to break with the past, to improvise, becomes in its translation to the situation of the sisters, an incentive to depart from inherited scripts and make new ones.

Debating Māori futures?

Grace mobilizes Dion and Atawhai to stage a debate about the merits of alternative approaches to identity and history. Dion, a young man who has left the community for the city, suggests some of the conflicts within Māori culture about what face an indigenous politics should present to the world or what forms of resistance or activism it should espouse. There is some distrust of Dion among the elders. His political imperatives though fuelled by the excitement of liberation and newly found languages and gestures are seen to be at the expense of more pragmatic interventions in the local. Dion is often, ironically, seen as too dogmatic for 'Dogside'. While he hoists his Māori flag in the city and decorates his walls with posters of 'Dread Beat and Blood, Lee Scratch Perry and Roots Foundation' (176), thus advertising an affiliation with a wider black politics, he embodies too a youthful Māori identity politics that hasn't yet matured. Indeed he is seen as in danger of becoming 'ungrounded' and because of that fixating on a distracting, idealized and perhaps less than enabling vision of the ground/force (*mana whenua*) on which *Māori* identity is built. Dion, we are told, lives off the ground, in a high rise block and what he sleeps on is described as a 'shelf' or 'platform' which seems to emphasize anxieties about his 'ungroundedness' or the possible forms of alienation embedded in his approach to performing indigeneity.

At the same time, he talks much of getting back to the ground. He is fond of hierarchies, of graphs of authenticity as amplified in his insistence that food cooked closer to the ground or to the fire tastes better. The word 'platform' itself seems to consolidate Grace's suggestion that Dion is performing a politics, a position that is just that, political, but not yet pragmatic, of use and value to the community. His strident performance of this position exposes divisions between generations. Those divisions aren't always easily resolved but Grace suggests their partial resolution, in Dion's growth into the values of the community, his pitching into the project to turn Millenium or 'Y2K' dollars into a new *wharekai*. The figure of responsible growth is figured also in Atawhai, the doctor who takes up the role of singer, who tends the wounds of the community in his singing as much as his philosophy of care. Grace's focus on music explores the hybridization of Māori culture, how it travels and absorbs cultures from near and far. So, Hawaiian, country and folk music all mingle in Atawhai's repertoire. Thus music suggests other ways of understanding the dynamics of cultural interchange, illustrating how a distinct form of expression often associated with Pākehā culture (country music) has been historically changed from within by having its musical forms localized and infused with Maori cultural values, meanings and rhythms. Atawhai is Grace's final word about what kind of identity politics is useful for the survival and continuity of the community; one that eschews damaging forms of cultural separatism or hierarchical essentialism in favour of an inclusive, grounded but strategic and pragmatic *Maoritanga*.

Pleasure zones and playgrounds – still romancing the Pacific?

What we call 'Polynesia' emerges as 'a geographic and conceptual category' (Keown 2005:1) from the history of European encounters with the Pacific. Since then, European and Western cultural production has shown itself to be inordinately attached to the idea of Polynesia as a new paradise as illustrated in the work of the post-Impressionist painter, Paul Gauguin, whose use of Tahitian figures and settings has been the subject of fertile and by no means unified debate. His figuring of the Pacific, like many others, in romantic terms, contributes to a vision of the South Seas as a potential site of (European) sexual liberation, one effect of which has been the consistent remaking of the contemporary global Pacific as a kind of 'pleasure zone' (Wilson in Keown 2005:2).

Grace persistently invokes such histories of representation in *Dogside Story*, as the circulation of global capital is progressively unmasked as reliant upon endlessly repackaged but disappointingly similar and simplified representations of local cultures, to feed a global market hungry for new variants of old(er) desires. Grace mounts her own intervention in such circulations of Pacific cultures, asserting distinctions between those who cynically trade in the commoditization of culture and those who strategically mobilize their material and cultural resources in an open and negotiated manner for the advancement of all. On the one side, we have the romantic novelist, Dawn Anne Brown, who arrives, 'in search of new backdrops, new characters, a new outlook, a different colour' (29) and the Māori fraudster on the make (Piiki Chiefy); both attempt to trade in culture to advance their own personal gain. On the other, we have the remainder of the Dogsiders who while manipulating and thus exposing external cultural expectations of indigenous cultures, usurp Piiki Chiefy's original plan to their own end, to achieve short-term strategic objectives that advance the community rather than the individual, and in terms that are communally defined. The effect of this contrast is to demonstrate the problems and possibilities represented by diverse expressions of Māori sovereignty in elucidating possible modes of engagement with wider economies, including a global tourism which tends to codify local cultures in diminutive ways.

ANDREW MCGAHAN, *THE WHITE EARTH* (2004)

Postcolonial gothic

Traditions of postcolonial gothic explore the continuing ramifications of colonialism in a variety of locations, putting to new uses an older repertoire of ghosts, spectres and troubling visitations to critically interrogate the ongoing relations between past and present histories, colonial and postcolonial orders. Postcolonial gothic returns to colonial history to enact and exact certain forms of settlement with the unsettled past in the present, excavating the dangers and values of recurrent disturbances and displacements. It thus documents the legacies of the past, their contemporary countenance and transformative potential. If ghost stories are preoccupied by possession, the postcolonial ghost story, as Ken Gelder and Jane Jacobs observe, 'speaks not so much about possession as (dis)possession, coming as it does *after* the fact of settlement' (1998: 32). *The White Earth* like Alex Miller's *Journey to the Stone Country* (2002) is a distinct kind of Australian ghost story and while it is conversant with the history of Australian gothic, including the colonial gothic of Henry Kendall, Rosa Campbell Praed, Henry Lawson and Marcus Clarke, it also represents a departure from it and other more recent modulations of the tradition in Australia, in the suburban gothic of Patrick White, Barbara Hanrahan or Peter Carey, or the indigenous gothic of Mudrooroo and Tracey Moffatt.

It belongs firmly to a burgeoning tradition of post-Mabo gothic. It takes as its subject the direct challenges to the contours of non-indigenous Australian belongings represented by the historic Mabo (1992) judgement, that revoked the legal fiction of 'terra nullius', the idea that Australia was 'empty territory' or 'nobody's land' at the point of European colonization. In the history of Australian settlement, the doctrine of 'terra nullius' long provided the justification for the expropriation of land, which many historians have asserted is both the precondition and ultimate goal of settler colonialism, its defining project. In Patrick Wolfe's view, for example, settler colonialism is characterized by a 'logic of elimination' aimed at replacing indigenous society with that of the colonizers, whose defining instruments might include massacre, 'dispersal', spatial sequestration (camps, reserves, missions, 'Bantustans') and policies of biological or cultural assimilation (1994, 2008). Mabo and the subsequent Native Title Act (1993), in resurrecting the prehistory of indigenous settlement, and the continuing purchase of indigenous possession, fundamentally disrupts the grounds of 'settler' identity, and the buried knowledge of the realities that attend this 'logic of elimination'. Mabo brings to the surface a set of troubling questions about the nature of the colonial past and it demands an ongoing reconfiguration of the ground/s on which and to which settler identities lay claim in the present. It is a fundamental disturbance of the bedrock of settler order; its conceptions of time, place, history and the vicissitudes of belonging. The forms of haunting that Mabo represents demand a reorganization of settler chronology and the idea that 'history' begins with European arrival, with 'terra nullius'.

Disturbance is the natural terrain of gothic, and so *The White Earth*, published a decade after the convulsions unleashed by Mabo, takes a step back into that recent history to revisit the moment of impact. The 'Prologue', set in late 1992, opens on a dramatic visual image of impact, as McGahan's young protagonist, William, playing on the family farm in Queensland suddenly sees 'huge in the sky, the mushroom cloud of a nuclear explosion' (2004: 1). Borrowed from a recognizable spectre of global catastrophe, the atomic bombing of Japanese cities in 1945, the falling embers herald not another Hiroshima or Nagasaki but a more familiar local tragedy, the remains of a field of burning wheat ignited by an exploding harvester that consumes William's father. His death signals the entrance of Will's uncle, John McIvor, who offers mother and son a new home on the more remote Kuran Station. There, awakened but also confused by the mythic accounts of exploration and settlement that McIvor weaves and, with the promise of inheriting the once vast station, the prize of the plains, dangling before him, Will comes face to face with its unsettling histories in a dramatic trek across its shifting ground. Rescued by McIvor's estranged daughter, Ruth, Will's return to the station is further disturbed by Ruth's attempts to encourage him to interrogate the costs of investing in the 'gift' (327) that McIvor promises, not least among these the costs paid by the indigenous peoples the station has displaced. As McIvor and Ruth angrily debate the veracity of indigenous and non-indigenous claims, Will oscillates between the two. Ruth's pressing leads McIvor to hurriedly burn the remains inadvertently uncovered by Will, charged too with the traumatic task of their collection, for the story they tell could become the basis of future native title claims. In the melee that ensues, Kuran House burns to the ground taking McIvor and Will's mother with it. Will and Ruth survive and the novel closes on Ruth's assumption of the 'burden' of 'responsibility' for Will, whose partial loss of hearing as a result of his neglect, is an enduring reminder of the continuing effects of his experiences.

Throughout the novel however, the resonances of catastrophe, summoned by the opening image of the 'mushroom cloud' and its falling ash continue to overlay and infiltrate the treatment of the aftermath of the father's death. If Will's initial likening of the cloud to an atomic bomb seems to indicate a perhaps youthful propensity to misread one thing for another, such confusion seems also to be a portentous sign of the dangers of greater misdiagnosis or displacement.

At the same time, the spectre of nuclear explosion is also a warning to the reader about how we might begin to misread the histories of place that the novel interrogates. While McGahan persistently emphasizes the geographic isolation of Will's childhood home on the fictional Kuran Plains, he is keen to reiterate the forms of connection to the world that belie this sense of isolation. For what happens on the plains have their origin in wider structures, movements, geo-politics. Whether invoking Hiroshima and Nagasaki, or the later testing of British and French atomic weapons at Kiribati, Murora Atoll or Maralinga (on the Nullabor), the image of nuclear explosion is McGahan's way of insisting on the ties that bind the history of the plains and colonial frontier to the regional, the national and the contemporary global. Thus he challenges attempts to render that history marginal and refuses to see what happens on the frontier as either isolated or past, to diminish indigenous 'dispersal' or to doubt its significance in order to reroute or delimit wider public discussion of responsibility, reconciliation or redress.

Such evasions were a notable feature of some interventions in the 'history wars' of the 1990s when the colonial frontier re-emerged as a central topic of public discourse because of enduring questions about the nature and extent of settler violence in the early days of colonial settlement. While this attention to the violations that attend settler colonialisms and their 'logic of elimination' aims at shedding new light on past events and their current legacies, it has also tended, as some historians have argued, to reproduce the frontier as a synonym for extraordinary violence and extreme lawlessness (Attwood and Forester 2003). It is a move that does some injustice to the ways in which the frontier can be understood, rather, as a site suffused by law or as occupying a noisy intersection between domestic and international law, where 'the mutual constitution of law, sovereignty and nation' reveals the stages by which processes of Aboriginal dispossession are transformed into an affirmative account of settler possession (Evans 2008). McGahan is attentive to these contradictory renderings of the frontier, notably in his dissection of McIvor's investment in the 'exceptional' achievements of the region's pioneering forebears, 'a law unto themselves' (128). His excavations reveal Kuran Plains as an unstable, animate and shifting field of meaning in which diverse histories collide, buckle and are transformed. Such a vision of the plains invites the novel's location too within a transnational tradition of 'prairie gothic' stretching from Canada and America to South

Africa and Australia, as sites linked by equally troubling and trans-formative histories of post/colonial unsettlement. The plains are exemplary of the 'haunted sites' that characterize Australian ghost stories, which though they may appear 'empty' or 'uninhabited' are always more populated than they first seem, an animation that extends 'downwards' and 'outwards', 'vertically and horizontally', marking those who are 'always passing through', the 'people who take the effects of those sites elsewhere when they leave (as they usually do), spreading them across the nation' (Gelder and Jacobs 1998: 31).

Both nuclear explosion and the history of the colonial frontier, McGahan implies, are too productive of a series of effects that can't simply be buried, and if left untreated leak out or live on to contami-nate the environment and those it supports. These toxic effects are recurrent, unpredictable, distracting, figured doubly in the novel's mobilization of concurrent themes to often different ends. The first of these themes is apparent in the novel's attention to forms of environmental exhaustion related to over investment in colonial tech-nologies. These might include imported models of intensive agricul-ture which see farms like Will's as 'a machine, a factory to grow wheat' (85) to the detriment of pre-existing local ecologies and habi-tats. This problem is explored further in John Kinsella's *The Hunt & Other Poems* (1998) and *Shades of the Sublime & Beautiful* (2008). McIvor insists that Kuran Station, in opposition to the farms that lie on the plains below, is somehow unblemished by the debilitating effects of such technologies and practices: 'This is a piece of country. It's not just about heads of cattle per acre. This place is alive in its own right. It has a history. It's growing and changing all the time. It breathes' (85). This animate mutable image of 'country' is however only achieved by a subtle replacement and projection that mirrors the 'logic of elimination' suggested by Patrick Wolfe, that is, by eclipsing the animation (life) of indigenous peoples and their knowledge and by projecting that animation onto the land itself.

The second theme relates to notions of physical infection and impairment that are directly connected to the first. Here, illness and impairment are differently configured by McGahan as the symptom and sign of the enduring imbalances and ongoing effects of the unstable operation of underlying and continuing trauma, whether of the father's death or of settler colonialism per se. Will's ear infection, his mother's recurrent illnesses, Ruth's 'bandaged hands' (376) and McIvor's enduring limp all articulate, in troubling ways, a series of concerns about postcolonial embodiment and the continuing legacies of colonial settlement. Its unsettling, rapacious influences are epitomized, for example, in the tumour that eats away at the bone and tissue of William's ear cavity producing a leaking 'necrotic tissue' (375) whose noxious odour fouls the air. Its invasive passage is only interrupted by Will's eventual release from the toxic atmosphere of Kuran Station with Ruth's partial intervention. McGahan's deliberate recharging of such discourses of illness and injury occurs at a particular moment of crisis in the progress of public discourses of 'reconciliation' predicated on notions of healing, repair and rehabilitation, initiated in the immediate aftermath of Mabo and accelerated in official and unofficial responses to the 'Stolen Generations' ('Bringing Them Home') Report (1997). Such commitments or, rather, what might constitute reconciliation's social and political contract were seriously under threat by 2005, as communicated in the seemingly intractable conflict during the reign of Prime Minister John Howard (1996–2007) over the provision of an official apology to indigenous Australians for their mistreatment. This apology was subsequently delivered in 2008 by Prime Minister Kevin Rudd, to wide welcome.

Seeing things?

McGahan offers a series of disclaimers and maps on the opening pages of *The White Earth*. The first disclaimer which is also a dedication, 'For my parents, whose life this isn't', is related to the second which states: 'This is a work of fiction. While the Darling Downs are real enough, the northern parts of the region do not exist as described here. This story is not meant to portray any actual place, person or event.' Both, at first glance, seem obvious points of protocol, concerned with defining the coordinates of engagement. However, the double and troubling force of these anxious disclaimers, which could be seen to drive a wedge between history and fiction, is that they also have the potential to unsettle his greater intention, to illustrate how the history of the frontier has formed and deformed Australian belongings and to illuminate the continuing role of a range of national fictions in that process. These national fictions are embodied in McIvor's attachment to a particular set of symbols like the Southern Cross flag or 'Waltzing Mathilda', and events like the

'Eureka Stockade', tied to earlier periods of radical nationalism or traditions of dissent. McIvor's clinging so fervently to the outward remains of this earlier history in his foundation of 'The Australian Independence League', in itself constitutes a kind of haunting as the emergent political rhetoric of the 1990s is newly enlivened, McGahan suggests, by the worn symbols of that earlier surge in nationalist sentiment. In part, the effect of McGahan's disclaimers seem to reassure the reader that somehow, the events narrated in his novel belong to another order of reality, that they are past or over, thus denying or curtailing the continuing force of history and its fictive instruments. Alternately, in overtly policing the boundaries between fiction and history, we could say that McGahan's disclaimers demand we re-evaluate the longstanding relationship between them.

How authors fictionalize history and the effects of that ongoing fictionalization for wider understandings of Australian historiography has been the site of tense discussion in the Australian public sphere, as the controversy surrounding Kate Grenville's *The Secret River* (2005) illustrates. Culminating like *The White Earth* in the revelation of a scene of massacre on another colonial frontier, along the Hawkesbury, Grenville's novel opened a new front in ongoing debates between Australians about the constitution of 'History', questions of ownership, and the ethical imperatives that might attend the treatment of the experiences of indigenous peoples in non-indigenous cultural production. Originating in archival research on the early days of Australian settlement, the novel's adaptation of a variety of historical materials and events fuelled anxieties among some Australian historians about the collapsing faultlines between fiction and history. This is a site keenly mined and managed in Grenville's companion piece to the novel, *Searching for the Secret River* (2007), which reflects upon her writing and research processes and invites her readers to reconsider the challenges and pitfalls facing the historical novelist mediating the demands of history and the exigencies of fiction. Grenville's account of the material conditions in which her character, William Thornhill, initially loosely based on her convict ancestor, Solomon Wiseman, might be implicated in knowing slaughter and emerge unpunished, if clearly diminished, probes the dynamics of complicity and questions of individual and collective responsibility, that are critical to discourses of reconciliation in post-Mabo cultural production. In treading similar terrain, McGahan's novel like Grenville's requires an alertness to 'the critical role that complicity (both as an act and as a concept) plays in drawing out the complex interrelationships between historical pasts and present' (Probyn-Rapsey 2007: 65), in understanding how to 'live with history, and in connection with Others' (65).

McGahan like Grenville peels back the layers of history to catalogue some of the myths that sustain dominant accounts of settler identity, those stories that 'settle into' the archive to distort and eclipse more various local and specific experiences. Like Grenville, he too asks us to reconsider the role of (historical) fiction in/on the social imaginary in interrogating the transformative powers of (national) myths and the peculiar costs exacted by investment in them. In doing so, he traces the corrosive effects of John McIvor's obsession with the idea of a pure or absolute possession, founded on an idea of heroic labour as the guarantor of inheritance and belonging, an idea sustained by the assertions of 'terra nullius' which 'clears' the ground for white imaginings, for the fantasies of a white indigeneity. Images of clearing are themselves overwritten in McIvor's account of settlement by a fascination with building (McGahan: 129), with painful, heroic but often unfulfilled *construction*. 'We build', Paul Carter reminds us, 'in order to stabilize the ground, to provide ourselves with a secure place where we can stand and watch' (1996: 2), and the 'monumentality of the places we create' is an 'attempt to arrest the ground, to prevent it from slipping away from under our feet' (2). In this, Kuran House is an imposing and deceptive expression of the Whites' monumental dreams of possession and an early focus of McIvor's attempts to sustain and restore the land as his rightful 'inheritance' rather then theirs. The Whites and their descendants, once 'impoverished aristocrats' (23) newly translated by the acquisition of land and power, represent both promise and betrayal, for it is Elizabeth White, the sole inheritor of the station, who dismisses McIvor and his father from the estate, thus setting in train the desperate dream of retrieval and reconstruction that propels him. By the time of Will's arrival at Kuran Station, McIvor has returned to the house but it slumps on the landscape as a plangent gothic figure of the ruins of colonial ambition, of the 'dead ends' (32) of settlement. It is, as Will muses, more like 'a derelict hotel' (32), an image that only serves to highlight the uncertain and temporary nature of its purchase on the plains below. McIvor's attention has all but turned away from it, and Will seduced by his vision of 'country', begins to see the house as 'the centre of something larger' (28) if equally unstable, inchoate and troubling – Kuran Station – 'a sleeping giant of a thing, native and alive and half wild . . . the reality of it, earth and rock swelling beneath his feet' (117). Here, we can see that Will's imaginings like McIvor's are built on displacements that are never secure, their 'swelling' always a sign of their ability to take new forms, to destabilize and uproot once more.

Alongside the anxious disclaimers, McGahan provides a number of maps which offer a rudimentary guide to the landscapes of *The White Earth*. Maps are, commonly, a technology of power (Foucault in Rabinow 1984, Carter 1987, Ryan 1996) and they play a particular role in the formation and execution of Empire, in both the imagination and consolidation of settlement. They are both political instrument and cultural text, organizing relations in and to space and disseminating ideologies, values and beliefs. 'All maps state an argument about the world, and they are propositional in nature' (Harley 1992: 242). While 'sometimes agents of change, they can equally become conservative documents. But in either case the map is never neutral' (247). If McGahan's maps promise orientation, the illusion of a real world onto which his fiction can be mapped, in effect they are of ambiguous value in orientating the reader, operating instead, like the maps that line the walls of McIvor's office, as a synecdoche of conflict, of the kinds of 'territorial disputes' (Huggan 1994) that demarcate postcolonial cultures. In the first map, the 'real' places gestured to, 'Toowoomba and Brisbane' are not central but remote, far off, out of the reader's sightlines, McGahan illustrating, in effect, how all maps gesture to a place out of sight, hidden from view while at the same time they attempt to recreate that view from a point of distance and in the process, centralize. Maps authorize perspectives, they are a product of specific locations, ways of seeing.

The second map promises readers a more comprehensive account of an area roughly mapped in the first. It demarcates the route of 'William's walk' across Kuran Station and it announces the role perambulation will play in the novel's exploration of claims to place. 'Walking' is deeply anchored in indigenous and non-indigenous epistemologies (ways of knowing) and ontologies (ways of being) as illustrated in a range of Australian films including *Walkabout* (1970), *Rabbit-Proof Fence* (2002) and *The Tracker* (2002). The novel explores walking as expressive of a set of complex and culturally distinct performances of relationship to place. Indeed, it juxtaposes contrasting and often contested accounts of walking the land (indigenous nomadism and European exploration) to delineate the nexus of claims to place in contemporary Australia. Walking is an index of indigenization carrying specific political resonances on terrain that is continually over written by the application of settler colonial technologies, as Mourid Barghouti and Raja Shehadeh illustrate respectively in *I Saw Ramallah* (2000) and *Palestinian Walks: Notes on a Vanishing Landscape* (2007). It is an activity that is, McIvor warns Will, not to be taken lightly, for walking is expressive too of other labours, that conjoin the human to the land that in their specific mobilization of the senses – seeing, hearing, touching – together institute intimacies, proximities, knowledges or what Paul Carter terms 'a system of memorialisation' (1996:12) that may overlook or override the ways in which the ground might have 'vibrated to the passage of other feet' (12). Walking can thus be an exclusionary activity but one that is as likely to enliven dispossession as possession, confusion as clarity.

In tracing Will's journeys across the physical terrain of Kuran Station, first with John McIvor and then alone, the second map's pattern of lines and dots invokes the formal patterning and pointillism of Aboriginal art. This 'borrowing' seems to situate Will's journeying as a kind of white 'Dreaming'. However, as one is drawn into reading the map in this way, such visions are disturbed, like Will's journeying by other resurrections. 'Borrowing' makes visible appropriation/s. The map draws our attention to its absent content, as the seemingly obvious referents of settler remains (house, village, station) are superimposed on a landscape emptied out of other markers, reflecting the excision of indigenous peoples from place, a move that must be figured as secure in order to legitimize 'white' possession, for as McIvor understands it: 'Possession was meaningless if it wasn't absolute.' (192) While McIvor recognizes, if selectively, a past history of indigenous presence and values the forms of purchase it had on the landscape, even while collapsing Aboriginal and non-Aboriginal visions of country, he is continuously compelled to reiterate: 'The Aborigines are gone. And that's the point. This is my property now' (209). Of course the reiteration of the mantra of extinction, the ghostly remnant of 'the logic of elimination', is a poor spell, easily undone. For McIvor, as for a wider public, Mabo unleashes doubt, as the spectre of continuing indigenous possession returns to upend his exclusionary narrative of a (pure) achieved non-indigenous settlement. This replacement of certainty by doubt, is embodied in the transformation of Will's journeying, less the consolatory white 'Dreaming' that the second map gestures towards, than a 'sleepwalking' whose terrorizing effects are signalled in McGahan's summoning of a characteristic image of Australian gothic, the bunyip.

The spirits of the plains

Will is 'caught' by the 'force' of McIvor's beliefs in an idea of country, 'that seemed to reach out like enfolding wings' (295), promising connection and relief from the doubts that assail him about McIvor's version of history, one which is increasingly compromised by Ruth's alternative accounts of indigenous settlement. McIvor's trenchant dismissal of contemporary indigenous claims and his feverish assertion of the veracity of his own claim to 'Native Title' leaves Will with a sense that 'something crucial was being warped here, bent into a shape it wasn't meant to be' (294). Still, he commits to trekking to the waterhole to seal his covenant with McIvor's vision and the promise of immersion in landscape, in certainty, held before him. His passage is derailed however by the disorienting effects of the ear infection that has raged unchecked since his arrival at Kuran Station. He gets lost and is prey to hallucinations, visitations. A series of dissembling if familiar voices and visions from the past assail him, enacting some of the brutal histories eclipsed in McIvor's account, but something else assails him too. 'A creature . . . a multitude of shapes, and no shape at all' who proclaims his origin in the dreams of 'black men' (316). Like all visitations, the bunyip bespeaks displacement as placement. The bunyip can be a cipher for the ghostly presences of indigene or non-indigene. Here, initially, the land itself is perceived as a kind of bunyip, whose disturbing and unpredictable propensity to alternately 'swallow' or 'reveal' the remains of those passing over it, serves to refute those attempts made to contain or secure it as the preserve of one over the other. It is perceived also as a site of intractability. As Will walks he notices how 'the hills' refuse 'to form themselves into a pattern he recognised' (300). Will's encounter with the 'bunyip' presages a discovery, that indigenous remains are not where they are thought to be, not in the areas signalled out by McIvor: 'No ring of standing stones, like his uncle had shown him, no ancient meeting place' (317). Indigenous remains, like the claims they substantiate, refuse containment. They cannot be sequestered like the local Aboriginal population, forcibly moved to Cherbourg mission at the turn of the century. They are, rather, all over. Ruth points out to Will the prevalence of stone axes 'lying all over the plains, as if they were just thrown away, like Coke cans' (282). Casualty underlines this litter, as Ruth reiterates, for such tools would not be casually dispensed with and constitute instead further evidence of the larger charge of forcible 'dispersal' aimed at terminating indigenous pathways. The collapse of Will's epic journey mirrors the fate of many of his favourite explorers; it ends not in successful immersion in the cooling depths of the waterhole but in the disappearance of the water to reveal the traumatic signs of indigenous 'dispersal'.

It presages too the ending of McIvor's vision and Will's eventual release from his seductive command in the fire that consumes Kuran House. But it is a release that is still riven by uncertainty and in this McGahan seeks to capture the enduring uncertainties left by Mabo. While Ruth remembers with some pain her interviews with the old women at Cherbourg she is no longer certain about what to do with the newly found information that would evidence a 'Native Title' claim, should they wish to make it. She feels both responsible and yet unsure of what exactly her responsibilities are and her hesitation reveals her own marking by the events that have unfolded, by a disruptive undercurrent of feeling, itself somewhat intractable, that she recognizes will also shape post-Mabo politics. This intractability registers itself in the stubborn persistence of her father's rhetoric of heroic embattlement and labour, which still hovers in her own decision making, in her seemingly conclusive thought that 'if anyone from Cherbourg really wanted the place, they would have to lodge their claim, along with everybody else. [. . .] In this world, something like that wasn't just given back. It had to be fought for' (375).

DIASPORAS 1 – CROSSINGS – MONICA ALI'S BRICK LANE (2003)

In Part One, I noted how postcolonial literatures are marked by a sustained attention to translation both as *practice* (from one language to another) and as *metaphor* (as a way of speaking about identity, culture, experience). Salman Rushdie's *Shame* (1983) critically mobilizes translation in exploring the dynamics of migrancy and articulating the components of a migrant aesthetic. Discussing the various translations of the poetry of Omar Khayyam, Rushdie turns to his own personal experiences to define the grounds of his affiliation with the poet, confiding: 'I, too, am a translated man. I have been *borne across*' (1995: 29). Referring here to his personal experiences as an 'emigrant from one country (India) and a newcomer in two (England, Pakistan)' (85), to which we might now add, with the passage of time, a third (America), Rushdie situates migrancy as fundamentally an act of cultural as well as physical (or geographic) translation, borne out or 'borne across' in and through language. He considers the peculiar challenges that migrancy poses to dominant accounts of nationality and belonging long preoccupied by the lure of fixity, 'roots' (origins). Drawing attention to how migrancy is often the focus of suspicion, envy or charges of sedition, Rushdie celebrates the migrant's flight (whether forced or voluntary) as an eschewal of fixity and an embrace of alternative 'routes' to re/creating identity, a liberation comparable to those bids for freedom that lead to the formation of new nations. Suggestively, he aligns the fates of transplanted individuals and newly coined nations: '[W]e have come unstuck from more than land. We have floated upwards from history, from memory, from Time' (87). Here, perhaps, Rushdie overemphasizes the ease with which the migrant might detach himself from the matrix of home/land, traducing the specific freight of migrancy even as he acknowledges the imaginative energy with which migrants approach the task of translating themselves in a new place.

I note briefly Rushdie's influential discussion of migrancy in *Shame* in order to foreground how Monica Ali's *Brick Lane* (2003) productively interrogates and complicates such an account in her continuing emphasis on the personal costs of such processes of translation for individuals, communities, nations. Excavating the contrasting experiences of her migrant protagonists, Nazneen and Chanu, Ali persistently registers the ways in which people remain attached to place and the challenges posed when the effects of such attachments threaten to distort or delimit the lives of others. So, for Ali, the question of continuing *attachments* and the various forms they take are as important as those processes of *detachment* that Rushdie foregrounds. In considering too how Chanu and Nazneen's children, Shahana and Bibi, engage with the migration histories of their parents, with England and notions of Englishness, as children of diaspora, Ali analyses the larger concerns that permeate formations of diaspora. Like Rushdie, Ali makes substantial use of translation in exploring the dynamics of migrancy, its bifurcation of the life of the migrant mirrored in the bifurcated structure of the narrative itself. This cuts fitfully between East Pakistan (later Bangladesh) from 1967 onwards and Britain from the 1980s to the aftermath of 9/11. The passage between the two is bridged by the letters sent between Nazneen, who migrates to Britain to join Chanu, and her sister Hasina who remains in East Pakistan/Bangladesh and who experiences equally disruptive forms of internal displacement.

Ali makes use of several other formal strategies to foreground the relations between migrancy and translation, strategies which cohere around the languages of the novel – English and Bengali – and the borderlands between them. As in Brian Friel's English-Irish play, *Translations* (1981), the central conceit hinges on the fact that for much of the novel, we are required to imagine that conversations between characters take place in Bengali, while the dialogue is rendered in English. So, one language always lies behind the other, emphasizing the new conjunctions as well as the forms of disjunction generated, such that, our own reading in translation, as it were, continually foregrounds the ways in which migrancy constitutes a living in translation. We are reminded of this too when Ali gestures to the characters' movements between languages or their imagination of other languages such as Nazneen's musing on what the Qur'an might sound like in Arabic rather than Bengali. Other insights are generated, as John Mullan suggests, when and where languages rub up against each other, as in Ali's frequent use of words 'transliterated from Bengali' whose 'English forms' are, he reminds us, 'merely approximations of their proper sounds – signposts to sounds beyond our hearing' (2004: 32).

This conceit is refracted in the letters that communicate Hasina's experiences of life in Bangladesh. The brokenness of the English/Bengali mobilized in these letters and their contrast with those Nazneen sends, suggestively embodies the fragility of such attachments, reminding us of the dislocations and mutilations wrought by migrancy and of the subaltern locations that Hasina occupies, but it has also presented several problems for critics. Many have discussed how the language, style and content of the letters could be seen to reinforce existing stereotypes of 'third world woman' (Mohanty 1984), making it difficult, as Michael Perfect acknowledges, to see Hasina 'as anything more than a symbol of subjugation' (2008: 11). Critics are also somewhat divided over Ali's mobilization of cultural stereotype in *Brick Lane*, the portrait of Hasina alternately framed as offensive, or knowingly ironic and subversive or, indeed, a deliberate attempt to create a moment of counterpoint serving 'to further emphasize and to render extraordinary, Nazneen's narrative of emancipation and enlightenment' (Perfect 119). Such judgements must be carefully considered and balanced against Ali's attention to questions of cultural performance and her account of the play of notions of (cultural) authenticity within and between the novel's diverse locations, for the letters do provide the grounds for a distinct set of contrasts. The letters juxtapose *locations* within diaspora, if, following Avtar Brah, we understand *diasporic space* as including those who leave *and* those who stay, 'who are constructed and represented as indigenous', as referring then to the 'intertwining of genealogies of dispersion with those of "staying put"' (Brah 1996: 209). The letters that cross between the sisters allow Ali to consider those experiences or positions (of class and gender) that might not change with translation/migration and that may be strengthened by the experience of dispersal and retrenchment that migration often generates. The letters facilitate an examination of enduring 'patterns of inequality and oppression' (Hiddleston 2005: 63) that continually traverse diasporic space.

The effects of such linguistic crossings and others like them is to reiterate how much of the self is carried or miscarried in and through languages, to plot the transformations that migrancy as an act of (cultural) translation generates in the everyday. Initially, Nazneen can, we learn, say only 'two things in English: sorry and thank you' (2000: 14), phrases which aren't just Ali's way of signalling Nazneen's outsiderness but of articulating too, something of the limited forms of purchase that she, like other migrants, are often afforded in their new homes, the kinds of performance (apologetic or gracious) migrant speech is called to supply. These informal formalities communicate the peculiarities of migrancy. Nazneen's English, if something of a disappointment for Chanu who takes pride in his mastery of the language, is also a valuable marker of her (cultural) 'purity', a guarantee that she is 'a girl from the village: totally unspoilt' (17). Language thus sites fears and desires; it locates the characters in distinctive ways. Nazneen's languages are an index of her movements between and within cultures and identities. They plot her changing identifications, affiliations and achievements, the passages of a new life.

Ali, like Rushdie, plots the forms of distortion to the migrant's sense of 'history, memory, Time' (p. 87), produced by the movements between worlds. If Rushdie seems to celebrate detachment, it is a celebration tempered by his use of the phrase 'unstuck'. The term suggests that such movements may be more 'sticky', that is, a more uneven, complicated and ambivalent set of *processes* than they first seem. This idea is prevalent too in Ali's account of Nazneen and Chanu's experience of living in a new place. For both, it sharpens their relationship to homeland distinctively; home is a fragile and mutable resource. Nazneen's sense of home is one that is, initially, immured in 'roots', in ideas of being 'in place': 'You can spread your soul over a paddy field, you can whisper to a mango tree, you can feel the earth beneath your toes and know that this is the place, the place where it begins and ends' (70). However, the web of filaments that maintain her connections to home are increasingly netted by the play of the passage of time on memory, particularly her memory of the 'village', as one form of memory is replaced by another, more elusive, tenuous, unreliable:

> It was as if the village was caught up in a giant fisherman's net and she was pulling at the fine mesh with bleeding fingers, squinting into the sun, vision mottled with netting and eyelashes. As the years passed the layers of netting multiplied and she began to rely on a different kind of memory. The memory of things she knew but no longer saw. It was only in her sleep that the village came whole again. (179)

Nazneen's relationship with Bangladesh and her memories of it are continually reframed and reformed by her growing affiliations to Britain and the alternative routes to the question of belonging that living overseas bestows. Like Rushdie, Ali is aware too that such reshaping of the past in memory can generate distortion, resulting less in the fragmentation of the image of the village as it retreats from view or from lived experience but its ossification in time and temper. Such distortions are reiterated in Ali's treatment of Nazneen's attachment to the 'story' of her own troubled birth, categorized in family memory as the story of how she was 'left to her fate', subsequently functioning as a kind of archetypal narrative conditioning her self-understanding across time and in space.

Chanu's relations with home are too framed by the oscillations in his relationship to Britain and the forms of inbetweenness generated by migrancy often intensified by cultural and economic embattlement, marginalization, nostalgia and/or perceptions of threat.

Chanu offers some rebuke to Rushdie's initial rather optimistic account of migration as inherently productive of liberation, for in Chanu we see the contradictory forces of change and stasis at work. While he is often dismissive of his fellow immigrants for failing to leave the village behind, impugning the continuity of 'peasant' ways as the reason for the trials that assail the community, at the same time, he continues to foist his own regressive prejudices, against Sylhetis, for example, on his children. Increasingly disillusioned with his life in Britain, Chanu succumbs to what his friend Dr Azad cautions is a terminal condition, 'Going Home Syndrome'. Resolving to return to Bangladesh with his family, Chanu invests the process of reinventing his belongings with the same imaginative energies he had previously devoted to inventing his future in England. In both the first crossing is in language. Where Shakespeare articulated the horizons of his early ambitions, the journey home begins with Tagore (146) and the recitation of 'Golden Bengal'. Here, Chanu's attachment to and reliance upon a borrowed, formalized, deeply gendered and somewhat overwrought expression of filiation (Said 1983), serves to reiterate Rushdie's earlier warnings about the dangers posed by the urge to reclaim and restore a lost place. For Rushdie, 'physical alienation' from the homeland 'almost inevitably means' that in looking back, emigrants 'will not be capable of reclaiming precisely the thing that was lost', they will, rather, 'create fictions, not actual village or cities, but invisible ones, imaginary homelands, Indias of the mind' (2006: 428).

The recitation belies a greater incidence of fracture, for while Chanu dissolves in tears, overcome by the promise of succour the song offers, the conditions under which such recitations take place installs a further wedge between Chanu and his daughters which leads to a defining moment of affiliation (Said 1983), culminating in Shahana, Bibi and Nazneen's choosing to remain in Britain in defiance of the compulsory return threatened by Chanu. His return to Bangladesh, while it doesn't overturn Azad's pessimistic account of the fatalism of such a move, does not confirm it either. He lives his life, as his letters to Nazneen indicate, much as he had in Britain, and if divested of the imagined consolations of return, he is imbued with a new appreciation of his family in their absence. Neither is this new departure a leave taking of family, but a reorganization of the arrangements between them and it suggests something too of the other mobilities that attend the crossings of diaspora.

Diasporic journeys, Avtar Brah argues, are 'embarked upon, lived and re-lived through multiple modalities' which include 'gender, race, class, religion, language and generation' (1996: 184). The modality of generation and analysis of intergenerational conflict are critical to Ali's portrait of diaspora and its hybridities. Her account of the experiences of Shahana, Bibi and Karim as children of diaspora explores their diverse locations and purchase on Britain. Like a number of contemporary 'Black British' and South Asian writers including Hanif Kureishi, Andrea Levy, Bernardine Evaristo, Zadie Smith and Nadeem Aslam, Ali is keen to expand our understandings of the ways in which generations of children born in Britain negotiate the multiple allegiances of diaspora, particularly in moments of social crisis which often locate diasporic communities adversely or reconfigure the relational positioning of diasporic communities with/in the hostland. 'Brick Lane' in London's East End is itself a mobile image of such histories, and in using London as a setting Ali resurrects the varied histories of representing London in colonial and postcolonial writing, as a congested site of multiple departures and arrivals (Procter 2003, McLeod 2004). Ali's focus on 'Brick Lane' also continues a tradition of exploring the East End, in the writing of Farruk Dhondy (*Bombay Duck*) and Manzural Islam (*The Mapmakers of Spitalfields*), for example, as a border space deeply scored not only by its histories of (racial) contestation and conflict but by traditions of tenacious habitation and reinvention, forms of 'dwelling' (Procter 2003) that do much to articulate the often contrary histories of British multiculturalism.

CROSSINGS 2 – CARYL PHILLIPS, *CROSSING THE RIVER* (1993)

'Within myself I contain many worlds; I want to embrace all of them' (Jaggi 2001: 7). So Caryl Phillips observes in an interview on the occasion of the publication of the series of essays (part-memoir, travel narrative and cultural review) that make up *A New World Order* (2001). It is a comment that echoes Saleem Sinai's famous proclamation in Salman Rushdie's *Midnight's Children* (1981): 'I have been a swallower of lives; and to know me, just the one of me, you'll have to swallow the lot as well' (1995: 9). Behind Saleem's expansive claims lies a plea for a more complex understanding of the variety of cultural, religious and political influences that contribute to the making of modern India and a protest against ordinations of a monolithic homogenizing historiography of the nation. Phillips too offers a personal assertion of 'place' over 'displacement' but he also registers in his assertion, the political climate that would come to dominate post 9/11, a climate in which the fertility of those multiple influences, allegiances and/or extra-territorial affiliations that attend individuals and communities in diaspora are the subject of renewed focus, suspicion and hostility. One of the more obvious expressions of a climate of suspicion is the continual refurbishment of the conditions of nationality, like the citizenship test, which tend to reveal the age old exclusivities that attend the production of national identities. Phillips' reflections on his own experience growing up in Leeds in the late 1960s and 1970s and his sense of the rules of inclusion and exclusion that frame national belongings illustrates some of the more insidious ways in which diasporic subjects are called to continually (re)cite their affiliation to a singular or monolithic version of identity. He notes: 'There was a stigma attached to being the newcomer; you were marked as an outsider. The society tried to impose choice on you: are you one of us or not? It's a very British conceit – membership' (Jaggi 2001: 7). This observation comes into starker relief when compared with the recent experience of the young British hip-hop and grime artist, Dizzee Rascal (Dylan Mills), on a news programme devoted to considering the impact of Barack Obama's election as US President (Newsnight, BBC2, 5 November 2008). There, Mills' confirmation of the importance of Obama's victory as a sign of social and racial unity and possibility is undercut by the intervention of his interviewer, Jeremy Paxman, who suddenly demands that he clarify his affiliations to Britain ('Mr. Rascal, do you feel yourself to be British?'). Here, the interviewer's assumption of a (presumed) unquestionable 'insiderness' facilitates the projection of Mills as an 'outsider', who is called, like Phillips before him, to clarify his allegiances, a process made all the more incongruent by Paxman's confusion about whether he is seeking the view of Mills or his hip-hop persona ('Mr Rascal') and his reliance on affective dimensions of nationality, on the requirement that Mills calibrate the extent to which he 'feels' British. Continuity as well as difference links Phillips' and Mills' experiences whose juxtaposition suggests something of how the celebration of transnational affiliations and alignments is often construed as coterminous with weakened affinities for the 'home' or 'host' nation.

Phillips' embrace of the 'many worlds' (Madeira, St Kitts, Africa, India, Britain, America) that shape his identity can also thus be understood as a retort to prevailing climates of (national) insecurity, particularly in America and Britain. He gestures towards forms of solidarity with other diasporic communities located, like the Afro-Caribbean diaspora, at the "global crossroads" of culture, and insists on the values of a "plural home" (Jaggi 2001: 6) while also locating the 'mid-Atlantic' as a particularly homely site, 'where you'd locate most of my life and work' (6). In this respect, *Crossing the River* (1993) is representative, tracing the enduring effects of a distinct historical event and institution (transatlantic slavery) precisely in order to reveal the variety of ways in which historical forces continue to shape contemporary belongings. Like Rushdie, he mobilizes translation as metaphor, exploring not just the specific experiences of individuals or communities in the diasporas created by the slave trade, but common readings of slavery as a 'black' story emphasizing its importance too, as a shared story, of the painful intermeshing of black *and* white histories.

Moving between the eighteenth century and the present day and mapping a range of 'crossings' within and between Africa, America and Europe, *Crossing the River* is firmly anchored in Paul Gilroy's imagination of the 'black Atlantic', a term devised to account for the forms of interconnectedness, affiliation and exchange produced in the extraordinary mixing of cultures in the traumatic crucible of slavery and its aftermaths. Phillips makes strategic use of the slave ship, 'a living, micro-cultural, micro-political system in motion' (Gilroy 1993: 4) and diverse forms of journeying to focus our attention not just on the official narratives of the 'middle passage' but the more unofficial ones. The familiar 'master' narratives (represented by the Ship's Log or Captain's journal) are subsumed in and rearranged by some of the more unfamiliar stories of the 'many tongued chorus' dispersed, yet united in the 'common memory' (235), the diasporas of slavery. Originating in an earlier radio play of the same name, 'fragmented yet held together by the father's guilt' (1994: 25), *Crossing the River* like Phillips' earlier novel, *Cambridge* (1991) anatomizes slavery in its terrible divisions and fugitive unities, its unheard losses and fragile insights, complicities and missed opportunities. It tells the story of three 'children' (Nash, Martha and Travis), those descendants of an (African) father, sold into slavery, across diverse historical moments and locations. Their stories are pinned together by and yet escape the 'dialogue' between the African father and the English captain (James Hamilton) who transports the 'children' from one world to another and whose story is in turn, divided by the inter-weaving of official and unofficial narratives (journals and letters). Two of the stories (of Nash and Travis), are also told, to greater or lesser degree, by their white lovers (Edward and Joyce). Phillips' aims to restore the occluded histories of black missionaries, pioneers or soldiers in different locations (Liberia, the American West, Britain during World War Two) and to explore the histories of intimate relationship between black and white similarly occulted or eclipsed in dominant narratives of nationhood and identity, in order that we might more fully recognize the variety of ways in which the past informs the present. For example, Phillips' reflections on the experiences of black American GIs stationed in Britain during the war foregrounds the differences between their experiences and those of the 'Windrush' generation (see Part One) that came to Britain after the war, bringing with them a different purchase and claim on 'Britishness' by virtue of their Commonwealth citizenship. Phillips argues that an attention to the specificities of those experiences can help illuminate and explain the particular character of post-war racisms in Britain (Jaggi 1994), a country whose changing shape he continues to address in recent works such as *A Distant Shore* (2003) and *In the Falling Snow* (2009).

DIASPORAS 2 – POSTCOLONIAL LIFE WRITING AND DIASPORAS

Barack Obama's *Dreams from My Father* and Mourid Barghouti's *I Saw Ramallah*

Barack Obama's fascinating memoir, *Dreams from My Father: A Story of Race and Inheritance* (2008), is topping book charts across the world, a success which is, no doubt, informed by the confluence of circumstances surrounding his dramatic rise as the first black President of the United States. First published in America in 1995, reissued in the lead-up to the Presidential elections of 2008, *Dreams from My Father* is far from your average 'celebrity' autobiography, although its sales are certainly benefiting from the attention that accession to high office bestows. It is, in the first instance, a complex portrait of Obama's postcolonial childhood, offering an insightful account of his troubled negotiation of the various locations (Hawaii, Indonesia, Kenya, America) and inheritances (religious, racial, cultural) that now inform his experiences. It is thus easily locatable within the genre of postcolonial life writing, a category inclusive of a range of related forms of personal storytelling that include auto/ biography, memoir, oral and written testimony, journals, diaries, narratives of incarceration, travelogue, ethnography.

Addressing questions of subjectivity, memory and history, life writing also interrogates the diverse forms of agency and authority autobiographical practices bestow. 'Life narrative', with 'experiential history as its starting point' (Smith and Schaffer 2004: 7) has long held a particular appeal for those 'with limited "political purchase" in a national arena' (2) where it often functions to enable 'claimants to "speak truth to power"' (4) for it can appear the most obvious way to counter silence and misrepresentation, of contesting or laying claim to history. The modalities of Obama's position (his gender, class and race) would, of course, complicate any simple reading of *Dreams from My Father* in the terms offered by Smith and Schaffer. Reflecting upon his (self) formation, Obama considers the history of African-American autobiography and the conventions that inhere in life writing traditions, noting their diverse forms of 'storying'. Like many life narratives, *Dreams from My Father* reviews dominant discourses and histories of citizenship from several locations. Other forms of life narrative often reclaim and remember larger areas of trauma and experience as is apparent in the archive of Holocaust and post-Holocaust life narrative. The cultural prominence of post-Holocaust life writing and the dominance of psychoanalysis and its accompanying explanatory models (of memory, mourning, trauma) in articulating its relevance, means that it now occupies a powerful position in the archive as a kind of 'limit case' conditioning the reception and interpretation of other narratives of trauma. The acute visibility of a Jewish history of suffering and loss, sustained in popular memory by a wide range of memorializing practices (including life writing) has had particular ramifications, for example, for Palestinian accounts of history, memory and place, as a range of writers and critics including Mahmoud Darwish, Edward Said, Illan Pappe and Ella Shohat have noted. Postcolonial critics point to the necessity of recognizing heterogeneous situated experiences of trauma and call attention to the specificity of past and present, local or national experiences of genocide or 'ethnic cleansing' in Rwanda

or Tasmania or Cambodia. They look to the development of historically and culturally appropriate models of reading such events and
experiences, as much as they seek to elaborate on the larger connections between communities of difference across time and space (Dirk
Moses 2008).

As instruments of individual and collective remembering, life
narratives articulate certain claims on the past and the present, forging 'communities of interest', enacting strategies of 'moral suasion'
and issuing certain kinds of 'ethical call' to their audiences (Smith
and Schaffer 2004: 3). The front cover of Obama's *Dreams from
My Father* carries the tagline, 'Thoughtful, moving and brilliantly
written', which indicates something of the elevated role of affect in
life writing as it invites and/or demands certain kinds of 'feeling'
(anger, sadness, shame, empathy), working to condition its audiences
and their modes of reading as it percolates through local, national
and transnational circuits of production and exchange. As Linda
Haverty-Rugg reiterates:

> In writing an account of one's life, one *authorizes* the life, claiming
> a kind of privilege for one's own account. Every autobiography is
> an authorized account. This by no means establishes that every
> autobiography is a 'true' account, but the aura of authenticity
> nevertheless surrounds the autobiographer's tale. (1997: 4)

That frame of 'authenticity' lends the genre an emotional currency
and political charge that often accelerates its commoditization but
it also buttresses the diverse forms of intervention or challenge to
hegemonic models (of selfhood, citizenship, nationality) enabled and
enacted within its contours. Dialogue with both hegemonic and
counter-hegemonic discourses of race and inheritance are, for example, critical to Obama's *Dreams from My Father* as he surveys his
encounters with a range of black (male) American writers like James
Baldwin, W.E.B. Dubois, Ralph Ellison, Martin Luther King and
Malcolm X and with the political strategies, allegiances and alliances
they espouse. Such conversations are welded to a wider quest narrative organized around Obama's exploration of his fragile but defining
connections with his Kenyan father, whose mixed fortunes as an
ethnic Luo in the predominantly Kikuyu government of Kenyatta in
the 1960s, Obama maps, in terms of its specific refractions on his
family. The excavation of the father's rise and fall in the theatre of

postcolonial Kenyan politics amplifies in turn the prehistories that have shaped ongoing interethnic conflicts in the country, relating to land distribution, demonstrating too how the unpredictable afterlives of private and public auto/biography constantly reframe and are reframed by the locations they address. I mean to signal here the variety of ways in which Obama's auto/biography continues to find new audiences, acquire new frames of reference and meaning since its initial publication as the narratives it excavates anticipate, converge with or are overtaken by the returns of post/colonial histories in the contemporary moment.

All autobiography or life writing involves memory work; the selection, organization, translation and interpretation of memory, itself often fragile, fugitive, unstable. The self is constituted in memory and memoir is premised on the idea that in ordering memory we (re)create a self. Yet, such acts are fundamentally creative; they produce as much as they recreate memory. Obama's opening remarks in *Dreams from My Father* reflects upon the creative element of his narrative while simultaneously arguing for its 'authenticity', in directing his readers to its grounding in a range of oral and written, personal and communal, acts of storytelling: 'Although much of this book is based on contemporaneous journals or the oral histories of my family, the dialogue is necessarily an approximation of what was actually said or relayed to me' (2008: xvii). Here, his careful acknowledgement of the 'approximate' elements of the dialogue recounted implies that the 'journals' and 'histories' are somehow more reliable, less partial or open to question, so Obama precariously balances recognition of his own mediating function and its transformative effects against the proposed reliability of 'contemporaneous journals' and 'oral histories'. Recognizing the potentially coercive nature of his own autobiographical practices as he seeks to impose a trajectory on events and experiences, Obama further indicates his reliance on strategies of 'compression', the production of 'composite' characters, and rearrangements of chronology in rendering a 'province' of his life (xvii). In doing so, he accentuates questions of mediation, translation and interpretation, foregrounding the artificiality of all life narrative. The interrelationship of fiction, memory and story in life writing is underlined further when he describes the ways in which his (absent) father is represented to him in the stories recounted by his mother and grandparents, 'each one seamless, burnished smooth from repeated use' (5), 'compact, apocryphal, told in rapid succession' (8).

Whether they offer the father as 'a fearsome vision of justice' (7) or provide a 'gentler portrait' (8) each represents an accretion in the 'myth' of the father, 'both more and less than a man' (5) for Obama at the time of his death. A recognizable product of 'family memory', the ensuing narrative explores the dichotomy between the myth and the realities of the father as Obama ties his own boyhood pursuit of him to the search for 'a workable meaning for his life as a black American' (xvi).

While *Dreams from My Father* specifically addresses African-American diasporic formations and inheritances, it is particularly concerned, given Obama's life history, with post-Second World War experiences of diaspora, with the transformation of identities on islands as well as continents, wrought by post-war shifts and movements. Transformation is too the defining concern of the life writing produced in and about the Palestinian diaspora in the late twentieth and early twenty-first century from Edward Said's *After the Last Sky* (1986) and *Out of Place* (1999) to Mourid Barghouti's *I Saw Ramallah* (2000) and Raja Shehadeh's *Palestinian Walks: Notes on a Vanishing Landscape* (2007). Transformation, as Salman Rushdie reminds us, is born/e in acts of translation and the life writing of Said, Barghouti and others testifies to the myriad transformations exacted by the Palestinian experience of dispossession and displacement, a legacy of the formation of Israel in 1948 which effected the uprooting of three quarters of a million Palestinians from their land. Subsequent upheavals generated by the June 1967 Arab–Israeli war and Israel's occupation of the West Bank and Gaza mean that at least 5 million Palestinians live in diaspora, with at least 4 million residing in refugee camps in Lebanon, Jordan, Syria, the West Bank and Gaza, according to the United Nations Relief and Works Agency.

For Edward Said, whose reflections on the Palestinian experience are critical to his wider accounts of colonialism and translation, the 'truest reality' of the Palestinian 'is expressed' in how [Palestinians] 'cross over from one place to another' (Said 1999: 24). 'We are', he continues, 'migrants and perhaps hybrids, in but not of any situation in which we find ourselves' (24). This concise formulation of Palestinians as 'a nation in exile and on the move' (24) with its emphasis on perpetual dislocation and movement is reflected in the work of the Arab-Israeli writer, Emile Habiby whose novel, *The Secret Life of Saeed, the Ill-Fated Pessoptimist* (1974), mobilizes satire, irony and farce to highlight the absurdities attending the particular conditions of living for Arabs in Israel, condemned like Habiby's protagonist by the violent conjunctions of twentieth-century histories and geographies to a perpetual border/crossing. Said reflects on the ramifications of these conjunctions:

> The stability of geography and the continuity of land – these have completely disappeared from my life and the life of all Palestinians . . . Thus Palestinian life is scattered, discontinuous, marked by the artificial and imposed arrangements of interrupted or confined space, by the dislocations and unsynchronized rhythms of disturbed time . . . [W]here no straight line leads from home to birthplace to school to maturity, all events are accidents, all progress is a digression, all residence is exile. (1999: 19–21)

Stability and the feeling of continuity in time and space proposed by the image of being anchored in place/land is replaced here by a fundamental sense of discontinuity, instability and the dislocation of cherished diurnal rhythms. While diasporic identities convene around foundational moments of exile (exodus), some share an emphasis on the notion of return to homeland and on historic rights to return as is the case with both Jewish and Palestinian diasporas. Conflict between Israel and the Palestinians is, like many other expressions of settler-colonial conflict, centred on the question of rights to owner-ship, possession and management of land. These 'rights' are grounded in a 'battle of memories' (Darwish in Hochberg 2006: 49) often cohering around specific sites of conflict like Jerusalem, the con-tested centre of both Israeli and Palestinian national formations, whose historic division well illustrates Jacqueline Rose's observation that 'Nationhood is not a right, it is a claim, agonistic, most likely to destroy the other' (2007: 44). The formative role of memory in the conflict and in the search for solutions to it, has led Said to conclude that a 'common future' will only be secured if both communities commit to dissolving their historic indifference to the hurt of the other in learning to 'think' their 'painful histories together, however difficult that may be' (Said in Hochberg 2006: 51).

Barghouti's *I Saw Ramallah* testifies to the constitutive role of memory in the articulation of Palestinian identities at home (in the West Bank and Gaza) and in the diaspora, and articulates some of the challenges and difficulties of engaging in such 'memory work'. He opens with a foundational image – a (border) crossing – the narration of which invokes the temporal and spatial disjunctions of Palestinian life that Said describes. The predominance of such crossings in diasporic writing resurrects both the originary moments of diaspora and the attendant and continuing border politics of nation. All nations, land locked or islanded, are differently anxious about national boundaries but nations born of partition are characterized by intense forms of border anxiety and conflict whose precise expression are often overlooked, given the historic tendency within the literature of nationalism to eclipse the experiences of both partitioned nations and their new creations (Cleary 2002, Kabir 2009). Postcolonial theorists of nation are newly motivated to address such eclipses given the material challenges and vast human costs billed by the partitions imagined as an answer to the question of settling decolonization and postcolonial state formation in the twentieth century (in Ireland, India, Israel/Palestine and Sri Lanka). Barghouti's account of his attenuated crossing of the infamous 'Allenby Bridge' between Jordan and the West Bank, occasioning his return to Ramallah for the first time in thirty years, wrestles with both the personal and the political meanings of that crossing. Key here is the bridge itself, a palimpsest of competing claims and histories, national and international, private and public (2004: 10). Barghouti's emphasis on the visceral experience of crossing the bridge amplifies the material effects of the burgeoning network of border controls, refugee camps, illegal settlements, land rezonings and walls, that interrupt and reshape the daily lives of Palestinians, the product of an 'inhospitable environment of superior military force sanitized by the clinical jargon of pure administration' (Said 1999: 19–21). As Barghouti's absence from Ramallah is a product of the painful dismemberments of diaspora, his return is inseparable from their remembering. Both exile and return are traumatic, ambivalent and in the hands of others and yet his narrative works to reclaim the personal nature of his experience even as it is constantly resituated within and against a wider public one:

Here, on these prohibited wooden planks, I walk and chatter my whole life to myself. I chatter my life, without a sound, and without a pause. Moving images appear and disappear without coherence, scenes from an untidy life, a memory that bangs backward and forward like a shuttle. [. . .] I am the person coming from the continents of others, from their languages and their borders . . . Here

I am walking toward the land of the poem. A visitor? A refugee?
A citizen? A guest? I do not know. (10)

Barghouti's account of the crossing illustrates the challenges of
adjudicating between the myth of return and the reality. The promises
of return as propitiated in the popular memory of diaspora (in the
literature of protest, the songs of Fayruz) are attached to ideas of
reparation, healing, reconciliation, embodied in a 'bouquet of symbols' (the village, the olive, the fig) (69) and their life-giving qualities.
The actuality of return necessarily and productively involves an
encounter with the contemporary realities that attend such symbols
as the experience of return is moulded by the pressures imposed by
the more fractious, intractable and intemperate reality; that this
crossing is marshalled by others, insecure, a site of continuing alienation and dis/identification as much as it offers familiarity and re/
identification. Return like exile is process, it entails multiple crossings
that are always, like exile itself, unfinished. 'Relief is not complete'
he notes, after his first steps on Palestinian soil, 'Desolation is not
complete' (22).

This return is too overlain by the memory of earlier returns, to
Cairo for example, and it is coloured by his growing recognition that
his 'relationship with place is in truth a relationship with time' (87):
'I move in patches of time, some I have lost and some I possess for a
while and then I lose because I am always without a place. I try to
regain a personal time that has passed' (87). Here, the acknowledgement of return as a slow, painful incomplete 'process' is catalogued
in the profusion of questions that punctuate Barghouti's narrative as
he progresses from the border crossing to Ramallah, then to Deir
Ghassanah, his 'place' of birth. These questions are often rhetorical,
unanswered or partially addressed but they offer a structure and
form to the narrative; they punctuate and puncture it. They invite the
reader's consideration of wider questions of history, memory and
belonging, but also accentuate the personal nature of the journey;
thus they enfold the reader but also suggest the precise unfolding
and refolding of subjectivities in diaspora. Further, in asserting
that 'Nothing that is absent ever comes back complete. Nothing is
recaptured as it was' (87) Barghouti continually underlines the
contradictions inherent in such acts of (narrative) recuperation, built
on the tenacious persistence of memory despite its fugitive counte-
nances, being too incomplete, fleeting, contingent.

In *Culture and Imperialism* Said reiterates 'the primacy of the geographical' in the 'imagination of anti-imperialism'(1993: 271), a view informed by biography and long engagement with the history and philosophy of imperialisms and their precise expressions in the literatures of colonialism and anti-colonial nationalism from Ireland to India. And yet his specific elaboration of the Palestinian experience as inordinately defined by dislocation accentuates one of the difficulties in current discussions of the complex character of Palestinian identities in diaspora. Said's emphasis on dislocation born of the continuing political urgency that attends the still unresolved question of a nation-state for Palestinians and the similarly urgent moral imperative to seek redress of the parlous conditions in which many continue to live, may be at the expense of recognizing the precise forms of 'location', 'placement' and 'attachment' that also characterize Palestinian lives in diaspora. This is particularly important for our understanding of successive generations born outside the territories and with no lived experience of Palestine whose relationship to 'home' is transmitted and sustained in memory (Mason 2007). Barghouti's *I Saw Ramallah* marks a critical juncture in representations of Palestine and the Palestinians in diaspora for it directs its attention not just to continuing 'displacement' but precise and differing forms of 'placement' (Bernard 2007) for diaspora becomes too a kind of dwelling, it generates forms of 'clarity' (Barghouti 73), affords 'temporary permanencies' (92).

I Saw Ramallah, like *Dreams from My Father* illustrates the relational quality of much life writing, where 'the self's story [is] viewed through the lens of its relation with some key other person, sometimes a sibling, friend or lover, but most often a parent' (Eakin 1999: 86). The distinctiveness of Barghouti's own experience emerges from its contrast with that of his parents, his brothers, and his son, Tamim, as his narrative stretches across three generations to encompass but not collapse localities and situations in time and space. His narrative traces not just his return but the quest for a permit for his son to visit the homeland, for the security of the 'right to return'. The 'long occupation' Barghouti suggests has succeeded in transforming Palestinians 'from children of Palestine to children of the idea of Palestine' (62), a formulation that echoes Salman Rushdie's earlier diagnosis of the dangers of creating 'imaginary homelands' in trying to hold onto an idea of home (against the fact of its physical loss or distance). Here, Barghouti's attention is directed at the heterogeneous nature of that experience for those within and without. The difficulties of entering into the experience of others disparately located in diaspora are excavated at Deir Ghassanah when the narrator reflects on the differences that mark the villagers' 'placement', and his own: 'They lived their time here and I lived my time there. Can the two times be patched together? And how? They have to be' (86). Barghouti's posing of this question, in terms that evoke with a ghostly precision, Jean Rhys' earlier, melancholic grappling with the question of displacement in *Voyage in the Dark* (1934) illustrates how the question of 'placement' is at once perennial but also recurrent, specific, situated. This point is accentuated in Barghouti's attempt to pull apart how specific 'places' (geographical locations) acquire meaning (through time and in memory).

As with Hisham Matar's portrait of his Libyan protagonist exiled in Egypt in *The Country of Men* (2006), Barghouti makes specific use of the telephone in *I Saw Ramallah* to consider the recreations of subjectivity in diaspora and the transmission of mnemonic links to the homeland. 'The Palestinian', he argues, 'has become a telephonic person, living by the sound of voices carried to him across huge distances' (126). If the 'Allenby Bridge' is one kind of lifeline to the territories, the telephone is another. Offering a vital mode of connection for Barghouti's family situated across the Middle East and Europe, the telephone 'bridges' cultures and locations. It suggests the possibilities of transecting established networks and orders for it is an agent of reworldings; it cuts across boundaries and borders to place and replace the self. The telephone, in surrogate fashion, facilitates too a certain peopling of his son's life through the stories transmitted across its lines. But it is also a peculiarly fraught mode of connection, for 'the displaced person can never be protected from the terrorism of the telephone' (127). Barghouti's account of its unscheduled interventions, the news it brings of deaths, quarrels, refusals, amplify the forms of interruption and invasion that the experience of exile imposes. As with all modes of communication, questions of access delineate the passage of power, hierarchy and inequality. Barghouti reflects how the telephone, once a particularly resonant mode of connection ('a sacred tie') between Palestinians' at home and in the diaspora, has become with the ongoing divisions imposed by the concessions and compromises of the peace process, a symbol of something more exclusive and less democratic. Now, 'the mobile carried in the pockets of the representatives of the new born [Palestinian]

Authority . . . antagonizes ordinary citizens' (110) who have less access to the easy connections and privileged networks that come with centralizing the limited governance won, in the hands of the few. The mobile is, ironically, less a symbol of the Authority's greater autonomy or 'mobility' than of its stasis, its ongoing powerlessness. It is not so much a point of connection as a figure of the dangers of greater disconnections in the networks that link Palestinian concerns at 'home' and in diaspora as the ongoing conflict between Israel and the Palestinians continues to distort the lives of the people, inside and outside Israel's borders. It exemplifies too the failures of the current peace process, in delivering security for Israel and social justice and meaningful self-governance for the majority of Palestinians in the West Bank and Gaza.

READING

Indigenous writers and indigeneity

- Kateri Akiwenzi-Damm and Josie Douglas, *Skins: Contemporary Indigenous Writing* (2002)
- Anita Heiss and Peter Minter (eds), *Macquarie Pen Anthology of Aboriginal Literature* (2008)
- Daniel David Moses and Terry Goldie (eds), *An Anthology of Canadian Native Literature* (1998) [Second Edition]

Postcolonial gothic

- Gerry Turcotte and Cynthia Sugars (eds), *Unsettled Remains: Canadian Literature and the Postcolonial Gothic* (2009)
- Mishka Kavka, Jennifer Lawn and Mary Paul (eds), *Gothic NZ: The Darker Side of Kiwi Culture* (2006)
- David Punter, *Postcolonial Imaginings: Fictions of a New World Order* (2000)

Diaspora and life-writing

- Edward Said, *Out of Place: A Memoir* (1999)
- Joseph Cleary, *Literature, Partition and the Nation State* (2002)
- S.K. Jayussi, *Anthology of Modern Palestinian Literature* (1992)
- Jo Glanville, *Qissat: Short Stories by Palestinian Women* (2006)
- Philip Holden, *Autobiography and Decolonization: Modernity, Masculinity and the Nation State* (2008)

- Bart Moore-Gilbert, *Postcolonial Life-Writing* (2009)
- Sidonie Smith and Kay Schaffer, *Human Rights and Narrated Lives* (2004)
- Crispin Sartwell, *Act Like You Know: African–American Autobiography and White Identity* (1998)
- Gillian Whitlock, *The Intimate Empire: Reading Women's Autobiography* (2000)
- Elleke Boehmer, *Stories of Women: Gender and Narrative in the Postcolonial Nation* (2005)

Representing South Asian diasporas

- Susheila Nasta, *South Asian Diasporas: Fictions of the South Asian Diaspora in Britain* (2001)
- Roger Bromley, *Narratives for a New Belonging: Diasporic Cultural Fictions* (2000)
- Peter Morey and Alex Tickell, *Alternative Indias – Writing, Nation, and Communalism* (2005)
- Ananya Kabir, *Territory of Desire – Representing the Valley of Kashmir* (2009)
- Radhika Mohanram, *Imperial White: Race, Diaspora and the British Empire* (2007)
- Gayatri Gopinath, *Impossible Desires: Queer Diasporas and South Asian Public Cultures* (2005)
- Anita Mannur, *Culinary Fictions: Food in South Asian Diasporic Culture* (2010)

RESEARCH

Chimamanda Ngozi Adichie's *Purple Hibiscus*

- In what ways does Adichie make use of the form of the *bildungsroman* in *Purple Hibiscus*? What distinguishes her novel as a 'postcolonial' *bildungsroman*?
- Explore the treatment of religion/s and the historical role of religious systems in colonial and postcolonial identity formations. You might find some of the following useful: Chinua Achebe, *Hopes and Impediments: Selected Essays 1965–1987* (1988), Wole Soyinka, *Myth, Literature and the African World* (1976), Critical entries on 'Christianity and Christian Missions', 'Christianity

and Literature' in Simon Gikandi, ed., *Encyclopedia of African Literature* (2003).

- Read Chinua Achebe's *Things Fall Apart*. Consider the connections and differences between his work and Adichie's.
- Compare and contrast Adichie's exploration of questions of gender, tradition and nation with that offered in other African texts like Ngũgĩ's *The River Between* (1965) or Tsitsi Dangarembga's *Nervous Conditions* (1989) or Angelina N. Sithebane's *Holy Hill* (2005).

Patricia Grace's *Dogside Story*

- Read the *descriptions* of the *wharenui* on 'Godside' and 'Dogside' offered in the novel and consider their relevance for an understanding of indigenous identities in the novel.
- In what ways is Grace's *Dogside Story* concerned with an idea of history as genealogy?
- How important is genealogy in understanding formations and expressions of sovereignty in *Dogside Story*? Are there any connections between indigenous conceptions of genealogy and that offered by Michel Foucault (discussed in Part One)
- 'To me sovereignty means having authority over one's life and culture.' (Grace in Keown 2000: 62) How useful is this statement in understanding questions of self-determination (individual and communal) in *Dogside Story*?

Andrew McGahan's *The White Earth*

- Why might McGahan have chosen this title? How does it comment upon or explicate the novel's concerns?
- Identify some of the ways in which the novel makes use of common features of the gothic novel?
- Consider some other examples of colonial and/or postcolonial Australian gothic (in any genre). Discuss the correspondences between any of these texts and McGahan's *The White Earth*. What do they tell us about gothic in Australian contexts?
- Consider the ways in which the indigene or indigeneity is figured in *The White Earth* and in colonial/postcolonial Australian culture.
- Discuss the treatment of history in *The White Earth*.

- Can you identify any other examples of postcolonial writing pre-occupied by maps (real and metaphorical) or histories of colonial and postcolonial cartography? Discuss the role of maps and/or mapping strategies in the examples chosen.

Writing diasporas (Caryl Phillips, Monica Ali, Barack Obama, Mourid Barghouti)

- Turn to Part Three. Consider the account of Avtar's Brah's ideas about diasporas. What use can you make of them in exploring the representation of diasporas and their communities in the texts listed above?
- How important are questions of form in diasporic cultural production? Pick some examples across different genres (film, poetry, drama, art) to explore with this question in mind.
- Research the contributions to understandings of migrancy, diaspora and their aesthetics made by a selection of the following – Salman Rushdie, Edward Said, Gloria Anzaldúa, Stuart Hall, Homi K. Bhabha, Paul Gilroy, Trinh T. Minh ha, Smaro Kamboureli, Roy Miki, Ien Ang and Lisa Lowe.

EXTENDED RESEARCH TOPIC – POSTCOLONIAL GOTHIC – AUSTRALIA

Identify the characteristic features of colonial and postcolonial gothic. See, for example, Ken Gelder and Rachael Weaver's *The Anthology of Colonial Australian Gothic Fiction* (2007).

- What similarities and differences can you identify between any of the extracts offered in the above anthology and *The White Earth*?
- Consider the usefulness of psychoanalytic models for an understanding of gothic. You could start with Sigmund Freud's essay on 'The Uncanny' and move on to a range of other work inspired by his engagements with memory, mourning and melancholy.
- Identify what uses, if any, *two or more* other contemporary Australian texts make of the characteristic motifs of gothic literature? To what ends?

PART THREE

WIDER CONTEXTS

CHAPTER FOUR

CRITICAL CONTEXTS

COLONIALISM, RACISM, PSYCHIATRY: FRANTZ FANON

Postcolonial literatures are preoccupied with the continuing impact of histories of colonialism and with documenting the varied effects of relations of power in the formation of identities. 'Psychiatry' takes as its subject individual or collective psychologies. One of its primary explanatory systems and therapeutic methods, 'psychoanalysis', is often charged with establishing powerful models of self-formation, sexuality, culture and health that act as a conduit of Western colonialism. Psychoanalysis and the discipline of psychiatry developed roughly contemporaneously with the consolidation of European colonialism, at its greatest reach and power in the late nineteenth century. They are thus often firmly, if unevenly, implicated in the dissemination of Empire, its forms of knowledge, structures of rule and relations of domination (Bulhan 1985, Loomba 1998). But, in their attention to mental processes and behaviours, conscious and unconscious, psychoanalysis and psychiatry also provide a set of critical tools and vocabularies which help us investigate the underlying structures that mark the colonial project, its histories and values. These are most useful when care is taken in their selective deployment and application (Loomba 1998). For example, many theorists of post-Holocaust culture work with models of trauma, mourning and memory inspired by Sigmund Freud (1856–1939), his interpreters and opponents, but their vocabularies acquire a specific set of meanings in their application to a named set of circumstances and experiences (the Holocaust), such that if one was to simply transfer those vocabularies to different instances of trauma, one would be in danger of traducing those experiences and applying inappropriate models to the site of analysis. In short, in universalizing and/or homogenizing trauma or post-traumatic stress, we distort its understanding and ignore the specificity of individual experiences. This is not to say that psychoanalytic theories are of little use in analysing colonial or postcolonial formations of identity, memory or culture. The opposite is true and a substantial, dynamic and evolving body of work fruitfully addresses such concerns. It remains true too that the modulations of psychoanalytic models offered in post-Holocaust theory have important legacies in postcolonial theory where they *have* influenced the generation of models and reading strategies attentive to specific locations, histories and constituencies as evident in David Lloyd's account of the ghostly passage of hunger in post-Famine Irish memory (2005) or Sam Durrant's address of reconciliation, mourning and remembering in post-Apartheid South Africa (2005). Indeed, in this guide, I have been suggesting how the vocabularies developed remain useful in gaining a purchase on the dynamics of identity in colonial and postcolonial locations. Here, I will be addressing some of Frantz Fanon's critical ideas in order to illustrate how his analysis continues to be useful in addressing the exploration of postcolonial identities offered in a text like Chimamanda Ngozi Adichie's *Purple Hibiscus*.

The application of a psychological approach to the examination of postcolonial cultures establishes ways of reading that interrogate the psychological effects of colonization and/or decolonization, on the formerly colonized as well as the still and/or newly colonizing (Ward 2007). These 'effects' are often the product of particular 'events' (slavery, war, famine, indenture, genocide, dispersal). The development of reading strategies for analysing such events and their effects constitute some of the common ground on which psychoanalysis and postcolonial literatures and theory, as investigative categories convene, yet they are positioned differently in their execution of such tasks, by the diversity of their histories, locations, practitioners and the methods they deploy.

Frantz Fanon (1925–61), psychiatrist and theorist, has been a central figure in interrogating colonialism. Hailing from the French Antilles, Fanon moved between his birth-place, Martinique, mainland France and North Africa (Algeria and Tunisia). His accounts of the psychology of racism and colonial domination in *Peau Noire, masques blancs* (1952, trans. *Black Skin, White Masks*) and anti-colonial violence, resistance and national culture in *Les Damnés de la Terre*

(1961, trans. *The Wretched of the Earth*) are informed by his various experiences across these locations; as a soldier fighting with the Free French forces in the Second World War; as a doctor constantly interrogating but informed by the Eurocentric biases and limitations of his chosen profession, psychiatry; as a member of the Front de libération nationale d'Algerie (FLN), pitched against the forces of French colonialism in North Africa, in the Algerian war of Independence, the subject of Gillo Pontecorvo's important film, *The Battle of Algiers* (1965). The latter experience generated some of Fanon's most provocative political interventions, on the appropriateness of violent resistance to colonial rule, for example. It brought him too into creative dialogue with a range of anti-colonial revolutionary movements whose strategies and histories many current postcolonial theorists revisit in seeking to account for diverse forms of terrorism and/or insurgency pre and post 9/11. Fanon's work has had a tremendous influence on the shape of postcolonial studies, stimulating and troubling the work of many contemporary postcolonial theorists. Not least among these is Homi K. Bhabha, whose 'Foreword' to the 1986 reprint of *Black Skin, White Masks* is often credited with its current situation as one of the most important anti-colonial and anti-racist works of the twentieth century, even as the particularities of Bhabha's readings of Fanon have led some critics to argue that he has reinvented Fanon to service his own theoretical needs. Those needs are broadly aligned with those of the intellectual movement, poststructuralism and its key critical exponents (Michel Foucault, Jacques Lacan and Jacques Derrida), inspiring in turn formative interventions in the field of postcolonial theory by Edward Said and Gayatri Spivak, as well as Bhabha. Energizing and enervating postcolonial literary studies in no small measure, their work has also attracted the criticism of a good many critics suspicious of the ease at which postcolonial theory seems to have emerged from and consolidated itself within the Western academy, where it is accused, often unjustly, of failing to pay enough attention to the material and historical realities of the peoples it surveys.

Black Skin, White Masks is a product of Fanon's rich dialogues with both French colonial history and European philosophy and it voices his growing concern with early applications of psychological theory to the predicament of colonization, like that offered in Octave Mannoni's influential *Psychologies de la Colonisation* (1950, trans. *Prospero and Caliban: The Psychology of Colonisation*). Mannoni's study defines the psychological effects of colonialism in terms of its creation of complexes, the 'inferiority complex' and the 'dependency complex', the first of which Mannoni aligns with the non-white European and the second, with the black African. His constitution and understanding of these complexes becomes a key site of criticism for Fanon whose subject is too the dynamics of race in the colonial sphere and the disturbing psychic effects of colonial rule on the subjectivity of the colonized. For Fanon, colonialism is a kind of neurosis (disorder), one that inaugurates a particular set of responses in both colonized and colonizer, ordering their encounter in ways that are destructive for both. Fanon's attention is directed particularly at the lived experience of the Antillean and the visceral effects of colonial racism. Informed by his own experiences and observations and acquiring a specific arrangement by Fanon's juxtaposition of different voices and registers, *Black Skin, White Masks* describes how the black man is called into being in racism, by the 'look' from the site of the other, a 'look' which sets him apart and denies him recognition as 'a man among other men' (1986: 112) by violently intervening in and translating his sense of self, 'for not only must the black man be black; he must be black in relation to the white man' (1986: 110). The mechanism of this calling in which the black man finds himself 'an object in the midst of other objects' (109), 'sealed' into a 'crushing objecthood' (109), generates a crisis of identification in which a totalizing image of blackness enters to seize and fix, to repudiate his desire for recognition and reciprocity on equal terms. Instead, he recalls:

> My body was given back to me sprawled out, distorted, recolored, clad in mourning . . . The white world, the only honourable one, barred me from all participation. A man was expected to behave like a man. I was expected to behave like a black man – or at least a nigger. I shouted a greeting to the world and the world slashed away my joy. I was told to stay within bounds, to go back where I belonged. [. . .] I am overdetermined from without. [. . .] I am *fixed*. [. . .] I am laid bare. I feel, I see in those white faces that it is not a new man who has come in, but a new kind of man, a new genus. Why, it's a Negro! (109–16)

In documenting the effects of this shattering of the black man's 'bodily schema' in being forced to redefine himself in the negative terms supplied by the white man, 'woven' out of 'a thousand details, anecdotes, stories' (111) of blackness, Fanon makes use of powerful images of bodily distortion and dismemberment to communicate the violent effects of colonial racism on black subjectivity. 'What else could it [this form of calling] be for me' he asks, 'but an amputation, an excision, a haemorrhage that spattered my whole body with black blood? (112). Such an intervention in the process of self-formation and identification is understood as part of a wider system of cultural domination that can produce, as a consequence, a distorting desire for whiteness.

The specific condition of native elites, educated in the colonial language/s (in Fanon's case, French), brought up to identify with the notions of civilization and thus of hierarchy carried in that language, provide Fanon with wider instruction. Incorporating a language, we often imbibe too its world views and in that act, Fanon explicates, certain displacements occur, not least of which is the displacement of the local (native place) and the values that inheres in its languages and cultures. The explicit dangers of interiorizing the ideologies of the colonizer and of accepting the culture of the colonizer as *the* site of value and self-worth, are exemplified for Fanon by how the children of native elites are brought, through education to identify 'with the explorer, the bringer of civilisation, the white man who carries truth to savages – an all-white truth' (1986: 146). Discussing the role of children's stories and comic books which, in the early twentieth century, are 'put together by white men for little white men', he argues that, 'little by little, one can observe in the young Antillean the formation and crystallization of an attitude and a way of thinking and seeing that are essentially white' (147). Psychologically, Fanon maps the processes of transformation and cultural alienation through which the desires of the young black man are reoriented into a desire for whiteness. Hence, Fanon's title, *Black Skin, White Masks*. As Homi K. Bhabha argues however, there is no 'neat division' between these terms. Rather, they represent a 'doubling, dissembling image of being in at least two places at once' (1986: xiv) of being 'caught in the tension of demand and desire . . . a space of splitting' (xv) that is the colonial space.

Fanon's project in *Black Skin, White Masks* is to find a way out of the destructive pattern of denigration, dis-identification and dis-placement, binding black and white in colonial racism, a process of 'disalienation' (225) that can be achieved by understanding and then deconstructing the damaging features of Western thought implicated in the production of a negative image of blackness as alternately, inferior, savage, cannibal, sub-human. This project includes deconstructing those models, like Mannoni's, that he finds deeply flawed in their understanding of the relations between colonizer and colonized. He seeks to mobilize resistance to artificial and false divisions of the world, in which black is characterized as evil and white as good. For Fanon, this process of resistance begins 'with a refusal of translation, of black into the values of white' (Young 2005: 144), precisely in order to facilitate the reorganization of relations between peoples in the name of reciprocity and equality.

It is important to recognize that critics are often divided in their account of how far we can read Fanon's analysis of the experiences of black Antillean native elites as a wider template for the colonial condition. Rajeev S. Pathe argues that Fanon treats the black Antillean 'as a type with analogues all over the world', as exemplary of the condition of those 'colonized by whiteness and European cultures, as these are mediated through the colonizer's language, institutions, practice and values' (2001: 164). But Ania Loomba cautions against such a broad reading of Fanon's mode, arguing that the forms of dislocation Fanon privileges are specific to native elites. In addition, she emphasizes the necessity of foregrounding how such experiences are also modulated by class and gender as by race and insists that 'the split between black skins/white masks is differentially experienced in various colonial and postcolonial societies' (150). If we stay alert to the specific conditions to which we apply Fanon's analysis and attentive to the problems that inhere in it as a model and build too on what eludes it or what it eclipses, we can expand upon its efficacy and usefulness in forging deeper understandings of the varied and continuing legacies of colonialism in postcolonial societies and cultures.

In addressing Chimamanda Ngozi Adichie's *Purple Hibiscus* and the still continuing effects of colonialism in a Nigeria marked by a fraught history of post-Independence political conflict, we should recognize the distinctions between the world Adichie describes and the one that Fanon pictures thirty years earlier. Fanon is writing *Black Skin, White Masks* before the great wave of African independence from the late 1950s onwards but in the light thrown by the recent rejection of the yoke of colonialism elsewhere, in India, for example. Fanon excavates the historical and cultural dynamics that attend the experience of French colonialism in the Caribbean and mainland France, whereas Adichie's analysis concerns a Nigeria that is still processing the effects of *British* colonialism, some thirty years after its independence in 1960. So, Adichie is exploring a particular time, place and set of relations with the (former) colonial power that are substantially different from the locales and conditions Fanon describes. Yet, in both cases, they are explicating the experiences of 'native elites', those educated in the colonial languages or invited to become mobile within the colonial system or its postcolonial avatars. Here, Fanon's descriptions of the mechanisms of indoctrination and the dangerous effects of internalizing the more damaging cultural values of the colonizer are still of use, if properly tempered by an understanding of the differentiations above.

Religion and education are key sites of cultural transmission and more problematically, indoctrination and transformation. Historically, they have been important conduits of the social mission of English imperialism (Spivak 1985), and exemplary tools of power and domination, as discussed in Part One. They have also been sources of agency, mobility and insurgency, defining sites of expression and self-realization for colonial and postcolonial cultures. Adichie's representation of Kambili's father, Eugene, offers us a powerful image of some of the more damaging legacies of education and religion as forms of domination, as technologies of power. Eugene's exposure to such technologies is established by his role as 'houseboy' for the religious 'fathers', an occupation that helps secure his education and wittingly or unwittingly, frames both his entry into and mobility within the colonial system (Adichie 2005: 47). The 'houseboy' or 'housegirl' is a resonant figure in colonial and postcolonial literatures and many writers have mobilized the place he/she occupies between spheres (private and public, colonizing and colonized, indigenous and non-indigenous) to explore diverse forms of encounter and changing configurations of power in colonial and postcolonial societies. Here, one might include the Cameroonian, Camara Laye, author of *La Vie de Boy* (1956, trans. *Houseboy*), the Sri Lankan, Romesh Gunesekera, author of *Reef* (1994), and the South African, Marlene Von Niekerk, whose recent novel, *Agaat* (2004, trans. *The Way of the Women*) explores the complex and deeply ambivalent relations between a 'housegirl', Agaat, and her 'mistress', Milla, against the troubled background of twentieth-century South African history. Adichie herself mobilizes the figure of the houseboy in her later novel, *Half of a Yellow Sun*. In oscillating in the spaces between, the 'houseboy' can often be seen to make visible the fragile relations or hastily erected boundaries between peoples across the divides of culture, class or religion. He/she also exposes the ambivalent, troubling and/or enabling forms of translation inaugurated by the performance or occupation of particular positions in colonial and postcolonial hierarchies. How ambivalence is expressed can also be suggestive of routes of resistance, Bhabha tells us, after Fanon, providing different ways of reading the 'agency' of the colonized and moving outside a totalizing image of his/her over determination by colonial power (Fanon 1986, Bhabha 1994).

Inculcated with Catholic doctrine and deeply traumatized by his degrading (sexual) humiliation at the hands of one priest in particular, Eugene's organization of his family's life, his attitudes and values reveal that he has internalized some of the damaging hierarchies and beliefs populating the colonial domain. He is indelibly marked by a neurosis, whose origins lie, significantly, in the structures and orders of colonialism, memorably evinced in Adichie's deployment of malaria as metaphor for the effects of Eugene's assimilation of colonial doctrine. Malaria attacks both the mind and the body and it is thus highly suggestive of the forms of alienation that Fanon suggests are a product of the violent disruption of the psychic identifications of the colonized. Malaria/colonialism is the underlying condition, the 'manifest complication' (Fanon 1986: 154) that continues to 'sensitize' (154) Eugene's engagements with the world, complicating and distorting his relationships. Turning away from the animism of Igbo culture, Eugene rejects many of it practices and practitioners, including his own father, as 'heathen'. His attachment to cultural forms of 'whiteness' (to white masks) are further embedded in his privileging of conservative aspects of Catholic ritual and doctrine, and his violent rejection of Africanized expressions of Christianity. The surety, certainty and authority he seeks in constantly mobilizing discourses of purity against the imagined corruptions threatened by 'sin' are, however, revealed as poor armaments against the forces of ambivalence, uncertainty, hesitancy that stipple his position. Such identifications with 'whiteness' are not easily achieved or sustained, as Eugene is haunted by the self-denigration and disavowal such processes of identification inculcate. His own alienation is rehearsed in the violence he inflicts on his family, as himself. That this violence is directed inward as outward is notable, particularly as it leads to the loss of his unborn children: it is thus a mechanism with effects that spread across generations.

The authoritarianism of the state finds a mirror in Eugene's iron rule of the family. Adichie suggests a continuity between domestic violence, the violence meted by the state and the continuing 'epistemic violence' (Spivak 1988) of colonialism. Eugene's neurosis is not unique, but exemplary of a still shared effect; the unstable, violent eruptions that characterize Eugene's authority are writ large in the actions of the postcolonial state and vice versa. Adichie however is keen to point out that alternative forms of identification and avowal are possible which short circuit the mechanism by which Eugene is defined. Ifeoma's reactions to the legacies of colonialism differ substantially and are shaped by gender as by race and by her differently accented location and experience within both colonial and indigenous hierarchies. While these are often recognized as conspiring in her oppression, Ifeoma refuses the troubling forms of self-translation and privileging pursued by Eugene. She espouses a more holistic approach to the divergences and contiguities that mark Christianity and Igbo culture, one that looks to extract the enabling features in both. Her position affords an alternative view of the forces that mark the new state even as her hasty departure to America, to escape the machinations of state power, exacerbates the sense of crisis leavened by its deadly hand at the novel's close.

DIASPORAS AND HYBRIDITY – AVTAR BRAH, HOMI K. BHABHA, STUART HALL

This section addresses key critical accounts of diasporas. It considers their place in understanding national and transnational forms of identity and belonging and discussions of hybridity outlined in selected postcolonial critics: Avtar Brah, Homi K. Bhabha and Stuart Hall. Originating from the Greek, 'diaspora' (from *dia* meaning 'over' and *speirein* 'to sow or scatter') was coined to describe the movements of occupants of ancient Greek cities into recently conquered areas in order to consolidate rule, thus conjoining migration and processes of colonization (Cohen 2008). As noted in Part One, the term was adapted in time to refer to communities subject to forced movement from sites of origin or settlement by catastrophic events but diaspora includes too communities formed from the voluntary passage of peoples from one place to another. Both sets of

movements are shaped by the marriage of capitalism and related processes of colonial expansion in the modern era which organized and
accelerated great exchanges of resources (human and material) across
the globe, a process continued in contemporary globalizing processes
and in the international organization and reproduction of labour.
The foundation of large industrial areas known as 'Export Processing Zones' (EPZs), sponsored by national governments to promote
foreign inward investment are instructive, in this respect. While creating much needed local employment they also often offer multinational corporations exemption from tax and labour laws and facilitate
short-term surface level investment in host countries. For many critics, such zones, employing over 42 million people worldwide, continue
older forms of exploitative labour (slavery, indenture) with very specific adverse consequences for the human and non-human ecologies
in which they are located.

'Diaspora' refers to the specific historical forms that the geographic movement of peoples take across time and space and to a
set of concepts, to the ways of thinking and critical languages
developed across a range of disciplines to elaborate on the disparate
experiences and effects on our common or differently situated ideas
of home, belonging, nationhood and subjectivity produced by such
movements. This cluster of concerns is often gathered under the term
'diaspora theory'. In Part One and Part Two, I briefly remarked
upon the contributions that Paul Gilroy, Salman Rushdie and Edward
Said make to our understanding of migrancy, diasporas and the
development of 'diaspora theory'. I noted a shared emphasis on the
transformative powers of migrancy and its role in the generation of
distinctive ways of seeing and being in the world, in the creation
of formative sites of translation and exchange, of cultural hybridization. Elaborating on questions of power and domination in the
creation of diasporas and their cultures, Said explains how such
formations need to be understood as shaped by the social positioning
of migrant communities and avenues of social power (access to property, education or employment for example) available in diaspora.
Equally, I noted how Said's recurrent emphasis on the traumatic
effects of dislocation and discontinuity, in his figuration of Palestinian
diasporas, is embodied in compelling images of severance from place
and time. Rushdie, I observed, seeks to temper his initial celebration
of the vicissitudes of migrancy as a strategy of liberation with a
more nuanced attention to the construction of migrant identities

as a complex and continual process of individual and cultural translation.

Exploring further the place of diasporas in discussions of national identity and the fortunes of multiculturalism, Avtar Brah's influential *Cartographies of Diaspora* (1996) matches empirical research on diasporic communities with a critical expansion of some key terms of discussion ('border', 'nation', 'location') in 'diaspora theory'. These intersect with and develop further the concerns articulated by Said, Rushdie and Gilroy. Brah addresses South Asian diasporas in post-war Britain and her work is informed by and adapts other influential theorists of diaspora such as Gloria Anzaldúa (1987) and James Clifford (1994). It makes several important contributions to our understandings of diaspora, honing further the critical languages developed to address both the experiences of diasporic communities and their narrative representation, the subject of Monica Ali's *Brick Lane* (2003), Nadeem Aslam's *Maps for Lost Lovers* (2004) and Kamila Shamsie's *Salt and Saffron* (2000), to cite a few examples.

Brah explores how the concept of diaspora challenges established models of home, nation and belonging dependent on notions of fixed origins (roots), whose potentially corrosive nature are explored in Salman Rushdie's *Shame* and *Imaginary Homelands* (as discussed in Part Two). Plotting 'diaspora' as a concept or interpretive frame, Brah emphasizes its contestation of notions of fixity and the obsession with locating essences and origins in constructions of identity by its foregrounding of the mobility, malleability and instability of (national) belongings. Arguing that diasporic communities are marked by a 'homing desire, which is not the same thing as desire for a "homeland"' (180), Brah defends this distinction with reference to the internal diversity of diasporic formations; only some of which are characterized by ideologies of return to an actual bounded secure territory, identified as a site of origin. She recognizes too, like Rushdie and Said before her, the often 'imaginary' or fictive nature of the 'homelands' created in diaspora, acknowledging the value of Paul Gilroy's observation, that the question of home is a matter of 'roots' and 'routes' (1993). That is, it is a product of the creative negotiation between home as identified with a fixed site of origin (a bounded territory) and home as mobile, as a product of dynamic recreations of self, community and nationality at work in the transformative processes of movement that solder diasporic communities. Home is a matter then of 'multi-placedness', an expression of identities that are in process and plural as Caryl Phillips' meditation on the diversity of his own location/s suggests (Part Two).

Acknowledging the shaping influence of the Jewish diaspora and its organization in traumatic accounts of exodus, as a defining 'model' in the field, Brah illustrates the necessity of developing alternative frameworks that recognize the historical and social specificity of other forms and expressions of diaspora and relations within and between (183). In this mode, her conceptualization of diaspora refers not just to the 'interweaving' of 'multiple' narratives of journeying, those different moments of migration in time and space, 'the composite formation', that we give the term 'South Asian' or 'Irish', but also the 'economic, political and cultural specificities linking these components' (183). As Brah uses it, diaspora is imbricated in 'a multi-axial understanding of power; one that problematizes the notion of minority/majority' (187) frequently organizing discussions of diasporas in Britain and America. This approach recognizes 'relational positionality', that is, the ways in which different 'minorities' are situated in relation to each other as well as to 'majorities'. It recognizes that individuals or communities may occupy 'minority' and 'majority' positions simultaneously or at different times given the 'changing multilocationality' (190) of some diasporic formations. Thus, it challenges the usefulness of the categories 'minority' and 'majority' by making visible the kinds of experiences such polarities deny. Irish diasporas in Britain, for example, historically constitute its largest demographic 'minority' yet, commonly, given the forms of racialization at work in the construction of Irishness in Britain in the latter half of the twentieth century, emphasizing a shared 'whiteness' with a white 'majority', the Irish are often positioned in relations of dominance towards differently racialized 'minorities', of, for example, Afro-Caribbean or Chinese descent. Such privileging of a shared whiteness eclipses not only the racial differentiations within Irishness but the long history of positioning the Irish in colonial discourse as the racial and cultural other (Young 1995, Eagleton 1995, Stratton 2004). It may also obscure continuing histories of racialized exclusion and discrimination and patterns of inclusion and exclusion that operate along other axes of difference (of class, gender, religion, sexuality).

Brah's emphasis on 'narrativity' in the construction and mainte- nance of diasporas is critically important for students of postcolonial literatures. While the interrelationships between narrative, movement and processes of (imperial) domination and subordination are a defining feature of Edward Said's *Orientalism* (1978) and *Culture and Imperialism* (1993), Brah foregrounds how diasporas are the product of a confluence of narratives sustained and reproduced in individual and collective acts of memory. She celebrates the malleability of diasporic figurations of community and the role of vernacular performances in their composition by drawing attention to the role of the commonplace or everyday in the creation of diasporic identities. She is not unique in insisting on reading diasporic communities as a product of narrative and ritual performances of belonging, as well as of regimes of power, nor is she unique in insisting on the importance of 'the materiality of the everyday' (183). But, in valuing the daily, routine or unexceptional moments in the shaping of diasporic identities she clearly pegs her conceptualization of diaspora to the 'lived' experiences of diasporic communities. In so doing, she responds to the residual criticism of some postcolonial theory for its 'abandonment of historical or social explanation' (Parry 2004: 4) in which it is also charged with producing utopian or privileged accounts of diasporic identities, or of eclipsing embedded structures of inequality which often continue to dictate the terms under which cultures meet in and 'after' colonialism (Ahmad 1992, Dirlik 1994, San Juan 1998). Unpacking the materiality of diasporic communities demands, Brah contends, an attention to their internal differentiation, to the ways in which individual experiences of diaspora are marked by the 'multiple modalities' (gender, 'race', class, religion, language and generation) through which they are lived. Consequently, diasporas are, she attests, 'heterogeneous, contested spaces, even as they are implicated in the construction of a common "we"' (184).

Brah's account of the heterogeneity of diasporic spaces is useful in analysing the portrait of diasporic identities offered in Monica Ali's *Brick Lane*, juxtaposing contrasting experiences of diaspora across generation, gender and class locations. Indeed, the noisy contestations and intersections that mark diaspora space are embodied in the internal vacillations of her protagonists, Chanu and Nazneen. Chanu's personal narrative of the fate and fortunes of the Bangladeshi diaspora in Britain is torn between condemnation, defence and admiration of the forms of (re)location adopted by the diasporic community and the tenacity of their diverse fabrications of home in diaspora. Chanu struggles to organize a singular or stable account of diasporic community, even as he consistently mobilizes the idea of a pre-existing narrative or shared history to counter the more dissembling images of Bangladesh that pertain in Britain, summarized as: 'All flood here and famine there and taking up collection tins' (Ali 2003: 152). Ali thus illustrates the diversity within diasporic locations themselves but also in how they might be read across diasporic space.

Brah pays particular attention to the border and the idea of 'border theory' as developed by Gloria Anzaldúa in her foundational analysis of the US–Mexico border (1987) where 'border' is simultaneously recognized as a physical expression of the underlying structures of power and inequality that shape the meeting of 'First' and 'Third World', as the lived experience (of the effects of such structures of inequality) and as a way of talking about other boundaries (cultural, psychic) and forms of demarcation or difference (of sex, class, race, gender, religion) that attend border/crossing. The focus on borders and the distinct forms of fracture they produce (self/Other, us/them, inside/outside) foregrounds questions of location. Here, Brah's emphasis on the question of how diasporas *locate* (within and without national borders) seeks to reverse a prevalent focus on questions of displacement and dislocation in diaspora theory (as my discussion of Edward Said in Part Two observes). Diasporas, Brah insists, are always placed.

Brah proposes the idea of *diaspora space* as a way of understanding the 'intersectionality of diaspora, border and dis/location' (208). This space is populated by migrants and their descendents, but also by those positioned as indigenous and so she extends the terms of reference by which diasporas are normally understood, to include 'the entanglement, the intertwining of genealogies of dispersion with those of "staying put"' (209). In *Brick Lane*, for example, this commingling is embodied in Ali's focus on the continuous imbrications of Nazneen's stories of life in England with those of her sister, Hasina, remaining in Bangladesh. Hasina is subject to forms of (internal) displacement by poverty, marginality and social stigma in ways that are proximate to but also substantially different from Nazneen's. In the letters that pass between them Ali foregrounds questions of transit; actual and imagined crossings of borders, languages, cultures, locations. The letters (like the telephone in Barghouti's *I Saw Ramallah*) make visible the continued operation, in diaspora space, of official and unofficial technologies of surveillance and control that can reach across national boundaries to condition the lives of those in diaspora. In the dispatch and receipt of the letters, for example, Nazneen often has to circumvent the interventions of her husband, mobilizing tradition and culture to police her relationships with family and the conditions of her new life in England. Extrapolating further, Brah reiterates, that in diaspora space *'the native is as much a diasporian as the diasporian is the native'* (209). That acknowledgement would allow us to appreciate the contiguities as well as the differences that mark the representation of diaspora in *Brick Lane*. Here, one might foreground Ali's attention to the modalities (of race, gender, generation) that condition Nazneen's encounters with others, notably the anonymous 'Tattoo Lady' inhabiting the block of flats that is her new home in 'Tower Hamlets'. Indeed, the flats are metaphorically both 'tower' and 'hamlet'; the habitus of isolation and marginality but also of social interchange and community, however confined those interchanges might be. Their intersecting location in 'diaspora space' should not be equated however with the idea that relations of power between them are flattened within its domains, for other axes of differentiation (ethnicity, religion) continually define the terms under which individuals and communities inhabit diaspora space. While Brah sees the prevalence of majority/minority discourses in figurations of multiculturalism as the product of particular relationships of power, her advance of the term 'diaspora space' offers a substantial challenge to centre/periphery, majority/minority models of culture. Diaspora identities are not minority identities, 'nor are they at the periphery of something that sees itself as located at the centre, although they may be represented as such' (210). Brah's vision of diaspora space works to undo the seemingly monolithic 'sameness' of the 'centre' by a concentration on the hybridities that populate and differentiate it. Diaspora identities restructure and reorient received notions of space and place, reworking categories and traditions, like England and Englishness, in the process.

THINKING HYBRIDITY

The 'entanglement' of peoples and cultures is related to discussions of 'hybridity', a critically important concept with a diverse set of applications in postcolonial literatures and theory (Young 1995, Brah and Coombes 2000, Ang 2001). Robert Young's *Colonial Desire: Hybridity in Theory, Culture and Race* (1995) rehearses the histories of 'hybridity' or intermixing across boundaries of race, culture and language. He tracks the term's origins in the biological and botanical sciences to its role in Eurocentric discourses of race that come to prominence in the nineteenth century which operate to support or trouble the project of Empire in various ways. Young explores how such discourses, addressing questions of racial intermixing or hybridization, articulate a range of fears and desires and disclose a matrix of fantasies that often convene around notions of (racial) purity and separation. The effects of such contrary motivations (fear and desire) mean that discussions of hybridity in colonial discourse are riven by ambivalence and anxiety. These are key focal points in Homi K. Bhabha's work, surveyed briefly by Young. Bhabha builds upon Fanon's earlier work on racism, colonial domination and those imitative forms of assimilation pressed upon native elites explored in *Black Skin, White Masks*. He argues for a wider appreciation of *hybridization*, a term that emphasizes hybridity as a continuous and unfinished process of intermingling and exchange, as a marker of resistances and transformations and as a sign of the agency rather than the absolute domination of the colonized. In emphasizing modes of resistance to colonialism and dramatically refiguring the forms of agency available to the colonized through his theorization of mimicry, for example, Bhabha complicates Edward Said's accent on domination in *Orientalism* (1978) and he resituates the lessons of Fanon's work for understandings of colonialism in postcolonial studies today. Young's interest in Bhabha arises out of his own explorations of the mechanisms by which 'hybridity' has moved across time from being a way of speaking about racial intermixture or purity to one that ostensibly addresses forms of cultural intermixing or fusion that trouble received notions of cultural purity or discreteness. Young explores how and why hybridity has been translated from one arena to another (from race to culture) in excavating its contemporary purchase in postcolonial studies. He challenges his readers to question, in the process, the ongoing interrelationships between race and culture.

Bhabha's engagements with processes of cultural hybridization, in *Nation and Narration* (1990) and *The Location of Culture* (1994), broadly intersects with but also exceeds Brah's address of the forms of cultural interaction, engagement and transformation that occur in and across diasporic communities and the processes of dispersal and dissemination structuring their interrelationship. If Brah is particularly attuned to the structuring of cultural identities in diasporic communities, Bhabha's work addresses hybridization as a wider organizing feature of contemporary cultures while insisting upon the fact that all culture is a product of historical processes, of conflict as consent, coercion as choice. Like Brah he is interested in the continuous and unfinished nature of interactions and exchanges across the border/lines of cultures and he celebrates the disruptive potential of both the 'moment of transit' and the movements that take place in the in-between, 'where space and time cross to produce complex figures of difference and identity, past and present, inside and outside, inclusion and exclusion' (1994:1).

For Bhabha and Brah, borderlines are spatial and temporal formations and they pose particular challenges to binary models (colonizing/colonized, West/East, local/immigrant) as vehicles for organizing and understanding the relationships between cultures. Bhabha's excavation of the complex ways in which cultural identities are composed and represented 'in processes of iteration and translation through which their meanings are vicariously addressed to – *through* an Other' (1994: 58), results in critically important evaluations of key strategies pertaining to the performance of identities. Exemplary in this respect is Bhabha's work on mimicry which contributes significantly to his sense that such processes of translation effectively dispatch 'claims for the inherent authenticity or purity of cultures' (58). Rather, he suggests that the discourse of colonialism and the binaries it harnesses (self/other, black/white) conceal more diverse forms of engagement within and across the borderlines of culture than has been supposed. In short, they conceal the heterogeneity of power in colonial space (Huddart 2006). Bhabha's emphasis on 'engagement' (a term carried over from his dialogue with Fanon) informs his understanding of migrant articulations and their performance of social or cultural difference/s which for him accentuate how the 'inbetween' might give birth to 'strategies of selfhood – singular and communal – that initiate new signs of identity and innovative sites of collaboration and contestation' (1994: 2). Figuring processes of identification and disavowal, sameness and difference, migrant or 'borderline' communities disrupt attempts to fix the boundaries of identities and traditions (our own and others) as stable, closed and discrete, revealing them instead as fundamentally split, unstable, unfinished. For Stuart Hall, whose work has deeply influenced Bhabha's, one of the fundamental lessons that diasporas elaborate is that identity is neither as 'transparent' nor as 'unproblematic as we think', for it is 'always in process, and always constituted within, not outside representation' (1994: 392).

As I noted earlier, Brah's insistence on emphasizing the value of everyday experiences in diasporic formations of community is a way of responding to the accusations levelled by some critics of postcolonial theory that many of its theoreticians overlook the material effects of power and the role of lived experiences. Similarly, many critics have suggested, in surveying the sway that celebratory accounts of cultural hybridity have held in postcolonial literatures and theory, that an over accentuation of the malleability and permeability of cultures can seem to contribute to a universalizing vision of cultural hybridity as automatically enabling, insurgent, non-conflictual and open to all. That means that histories of coercion or resistance, or indeed the ossification or fixity of cultures can drop out of the picture in the advancement of notions of 'happy hybridities' (benign and often false visions of multicultural harmony).

Brick Lane directly addresses questions of cultural hybridization and exchange. Ali's exploration of the different ways in which members of diasporic communities position themselves in relation to home, place and tradition illustrate how cultures might strategically resist the potential dissolution or reframing of cultural norms posed by processes of hybridization, precisely in order to maintain keenly felt attachments to place and culture. Ali exposes how diasporas might perpetuate highly regulated forms of tradition and culture *as well as* fostering new forms of cultural engagement and exchange. Social and economic marginalization and/or distance may result in the promotion of ossified notions of tradition that eclipse their historic 'mixedness' or internal differentiation in favour of the idea of a singular pure culture or tradition. Both Chanu and Karim are prone to such moments although their various attempts to take refuge in narrow accounts of tradition, religion or culture are, as Ali frames it, unstable and insecure. The effects of such investments are however productive of internal conflicts that shape their individual choices, their sense of filiation and the forms of affiliation (Said 1983) they pursue. At the same time, those conflicts and the means by which they are expressed and resolved, whether peacefully or violently, are mirrored differently across families and communities in diaspora. It is worth noting the particular attention Ali pays to everyday but often highly charged cultural pathways and traditions (e.g. of food and dress), to explore further the variety of questions that attend experiences of cultural hybridity, exchange and intergenerational conflict in diaspora space.

While Ali works hard to resist the temptations of 'happy hybridity', such visions do often fail to pay close attention to how hybridity (racial and cultural) and hybrid cultural forms (food, dress, music, fashion, film) can and are co-opted in the service of reigning structures, discourses and circuits of power (Shohat 1992, Ang 2001). Ali's novel exhibits a clear awareness of the forms of commodification and exchange that might underpin discourses of (happy) hybridity, not least in her choice of *Brick Lane* and its surrounds as location. Its 'colourful' and 'busy' conglomeration of shops and restaurants has often been positioned as a highly visible marker of a bustling cosmopolitan multiculturalism, an image that Ali is keen to unearth further for what it both conceals and reveals about the diverse economies and hierarchies of exchange that mark popular discourses of hybridity. In staying alert to the operations of power and committed to challenging its abuses, we remain true too to the energies that Stuart Hall, Homi K. Bhabha and Paul Gilroy invest, in hybridization as a continuing process of transformation and exchange, in undoing dominant formations from the inside out, reorganizing relations of power and recognizing and valuing difference.

INDIGENOUS IDENTITIES – CONTEXTS

Indigenous formations and representations of identity demand situated critical frameworks of understanding attuned to the particularities of their locations within and without the nation, alert too, to the ways in which they are both grounded (in specific cosmogonies of land and place) and also mobile, dynamic, shifting sites of meaning. Reflecting on the challenges in developing comparative models for indigenous literary study, Alice Te Punga Somerville poses the question: 'Is the term "Indigenous" a substitute term for "Maori" or is it an umbrella category – a context – of which Maori is a part?' (2007: 20) Speculatively, one might begin to answer this question by first considering a few others: How have such terms originated? What relationship do they have to a range of other distinguishing terms like 'Fourth World', 'Aboriginal', 'First Nations' or 'Native American'? Who uses such assignations and why? How do such terms enable or limit? Somerville's question turns our attention to the relationship between 'indigenous' as the signifier of a *broad coalition of peoples, claims, interests and cultures*, and the seemingly more specific cohort, Māori, within that coalition. In doing so, she asks us to reflect on the purposes that particular forms of naming serve and thus foregrounds, like a range of other critics, the fraught role of history, location and power in claiming indigeneity, Māoriness (Māoritanga) or Aboriginality (Rika-Heke 1997, Fee 2006, Huggins 2003, Moreton-Robinson 2003, Paradies 2006).

What 'Māori' means has been constantly reshaped by different constituencies invested in its meaning just as 'Aboriginal' or 'First Nations' has. This is evident in the constant shifting of the terms themselves in and across postcolonial locations, in how 'First Nations' or 'Inuit' replaces terms like 'Indian' or 'Eskimo', for example, and in the increased currency of 'indigenous' as a marker of a distinctly powered transnational identity, reflecting the ongoing social, political or cultural assertion of indigenous peoples. While Māori is widely used as a collective term to distinguish indigenous peoples of Aotearoa/ New Zealand, its usage is a legacy of European encounter and the histories of (racialized) demarcation that attended colonization, for, as many have noted, Māori were more likely to define themselves by *hapu* or *iwi* (tribe and clan group) affiliations prior to European inter-vention (Williams 1997, Allen 2002, Orr 2006). One of the features of settler colonialism in Aotearoa/New Zealand and Australia was a tendency to 'collectivize' and thus homogenize internal differentiations pre-existing colonization. Where differentiation was recognized it was often allied with newly imposed hierarchies that interrupted extant orders, privileging some aspects of identity and eliding others. In Australia, for example, official distinctions between Aborigines were often organized around categories of descent ('half-caste', 'full-blood') indebted to the (racialized) discriminations of colonial discourse. These distinctions informed official *doctrines* of assimila-tion interpreted by government in particular ways in their promotion of diverse *practices* of assimilation (including the controversial practice of child removal that marks the experiences of the 'stolen generations') which at once recognized and/or cultivated notions of difference but at the same time suppressed them.

In Australia as in New Zealand, Canada and South Africa, such organized interventions in the life of indigenous peoples, allied with the production and circulation of Eurocentric images and narratives of indigeneity (of what it means to be 'native') often operated in the service of the colonizers and were critical to the imagination and sus-tenance of postcolonial settler identities (Goldie 1989, McLean 1998). The effects of the often genocidal histories of settler colonialisms are embodied in recent debates about nomenclature (naming) in specific ways, given the acute awareness among indigenous of the adverse uses to which past structures of definition have been pressed, in appropriating indigenous land and resources and legitimating invasion and settlement. Some of these policies continued until recently, others continue in a different form today (Watson 2009b). For example, while some substantial progress has been made on the question of land reform and indigenous land rights in various locations (Canada, New Zealand, Australia, South Africa) in others, privatization of once public resources like water (in India) and land (in China, Mexico, Namibia, Botswana, Kenya) continues apace with minimal recognition of indigenous needs or rights. Extant and continuing histories of appropriation and exploitation, of indigenous peoples and of their resources (material, spiritual, cultural), suggest that how critics engage with indigeneity must be informed by the diverse understandings that such histories bequeath and the urgent political and ethical challenge for strategies of engagement that recognize but intervene in and delimit the perpetuation of such histories.

For indigenous, the struggle to refashion terms (like 'indigenous' or 'Aboriginal'), as a sign of 'honour' and 'strength' (Rika-Heke 1997) and to reassert the distinct values and resilience of the places, knowledges, cultures, and law of indigenous communities, has been both urgent and fraught. Such refashionings are a product of specific dialogues *within* and *between* distinctly placed cultures in different locations. Discourses of 'indigeneity' (of what it means to be 'indigenous') are shaped by transnational and 'trans-Indigenous' (Allen 2002) connections as well as by the forms of contest and intervention mounted at local and national levels. As a recognized forum for coalition and as a historic site for the exploration of such connections between indigenous, the United Nations (UN) offers a working account of 'indigenous communities, nations and peoples' that is a product of dialogues across some thirty years. Its official documents map a set of base coordinates for understanding what demarcates indigenous peoples; less a 'universal definition' than a matrix of possible commonalities. These recognize indigenous as those populations 'having a historical continuity with pre-invasion and precolonial societies that developed on their territories, [and who] consider themselves distinct from other sectors of the societies now prevailing on those territories, or parts of them' (Cobo 1986). Numbering 370 million worldwide, the UN recognizes that such groupings often constitute 'non-dominant sectors of society' who are, nevertheless, united by a commitment to 'preserve, develop and transmit to future generations their ancestral territories, and their ethnic identity, as the basis of their continued existence as peoples, in accordance with their own cultural patterns, social institutions and legal system' (Cobo 1986). Historical continuity might include a history of occupation of a particular territory or common ancestry with occupants of a territory, shared language, cultural expression or spiritual belief. In the UN's account, membership of an indigenous group is secured either through individual self-identification on the basis of some of the common ties denoted above and/or by group recognition and acceptance. These coordinates are developed further in the 'Declaration on the Rights of Indigenous Peoples', adopted by 143 nations in September 2007. Its adoption was opposed by the United States, Australia, Canada and New Zealand, although Australia has subsequently endorsed the declaration (April 2009). While this document is non-binding (having no legal power), it establishes an important set of standards by which states may be judged in their execution of their responsibilities to their citizens.

As many critics have observed, whatever the consensus achieved by such formulations, the politics of defining, articulating and negotiating indigeneity, individually and communally, is often a site of radical contest related to the relatively recent nature of *current forms* of organized intervention by indigenous peoples in the political and cultural arena, where the creation of effective forms of political community aimed at securing rights or defining responsibilities, has often necessitated the advance of a notion of a common core identity (the UN documents discussed above are one expression of this). As James Clifford suggests, 'commonality' is often 'historically contingent, though no less real for all that' (2006: 180). In both Australia and New Zealand, the 1970s is a key moment of indigenous coalition around questions of political and cultural self-determination and of decolonization. This is a project that is influenced by the specific challenges facing indigenous peoples for whom the 'postcolonial' is often differently accented than it is for other citizens, both in settler states and in states that were formerly colonies of occupation (India, Sri Lanka, parts of Africa). For many indigenous, the break up of Empire and the wave of political independence achieved post-1945 has not always signalled the end of oppressive structures of rule but their continuation in similar, different or more entrenched forms. The emergence of discrete bodies of indigenous writing in English is allied with the struggles of indigenous peoples for greater recognition of their claims to place, their rights to self-determination and the distinctiveness of their legal, political and cultural traditions.

Reflecting on what this means for formulations of indigeneity today, Yin C. Paradies notes: 'In the indigenous community we have only recently begun to demarcate *our own space* in which to debate the nature of indigeneity in Australia' (2006: 355, my italics). In accentuating the recentness of the critical and cultural project to demarcate our 'own space', Paradies also recognizes the considerably longer project of wresting the powers of self-definition from the stranglehold of non-indigenous. This is a precursor to his mapping of the dangers apparent in essentialist accounts of indigeneity that have the effect of marginalizing or alienating some indigenous (particularly those who also wish to stake a claim on their Anglo, European or Asian inheritances). He asserts the value of adopting an approach to indigeneity that actively seeks to avoid 'imprisoning' it as 'a fixed, frozen category of being' (2006: 361). For fixing 'indigeneity' whether by cultivating an idea of it as synonymous with 'suffering' or with 'marginality' rehearses a notion of the indigene as victim; it compounds a notion of the indigene and of indigeneity as wholly determined by colonial history and it overlooks the historic resilience of indigenous cultures (see Ashcroft in Part One). In short, Paradies addresses some of the dangers of replicating *within* indigenous dialogues about indigeneity, divisive strategies aimed at securing the idea of an 'authentic' or 'inauthentic' indigene which often work to obscure the ways in which indigeneity is a dynamic mobile category of identity and indigenous cultures themselves, living, breathing changing ones (Fee 1989, Griffiths 1994, Clifford 2006). Alongside some other indigenous critics he reiterates the shared and fluid nature of indigeneity, as a product of the intersubjective relations of 'indigenous' and 'non-indigenous'; an idea that is not universally accepted but often a site too of contest.

In attending to such contexts and contests and in cultivating an understanding of the ways in which dialogue on indigeneity might be led *by indigenous peoples* (writers, activists, critics) in the first instance, you might begin to consider further the *locations* (geographic, institutional, racial, gendered) from which you 'read' and how such locations shape the expectations and reading strategies you bring to bear on indigenous writing or other forms of cultural production (Brewster 1996, 2005, Hoy 2001, Huggan 2001). What are you 'reading' indigenous cultural production for? What are the limits of the knowledges you use to interpret indigenous texts? How are traditions of indigenous writing in English (life writing, drama, poetry) anchored in and informed by knowledges, traditions, laws and protocols that speak to and of diverse audiences and/or demand a reshaping of individual and communal reading strategies? How might their significant interventions in imported literary forms and genres (like autobiography and life writing) be shaped by local cultural conventions and traditions of oratory and story? Such questions contribute to the critical task of engaging with indigeneity on newly configured terms.

Continuing the consideration of indigenous accounts of sovereignty introduced in Part One, I explore further some indigenous articulations of sovereignty and of the particular role of land and 'country' in indigenous ontology and epistemologies. I do so in order to illustrate how such articulations might distinctively inform the work of indigenous writers like Patrica Grace (Aotearoa/ New Zealand, Part Two) or Alexis Wright (Australia) or Jeanette Armstrong (Canada) but also to assert how such knowledge might necessarily reshape and complicate how we read the work of non-indigenous writers engaged with the indigene or the question of indigeneity like Andrew McGahan (Part Two) or Gail Anderson-D'argatz (Canada) or Damon Galgut (South Africa).

SOVEREIGNTY

In a recent interview, Patricia Grace, author of *Dogside Story* (see Part Two) delineates her personal sense of what sovereignty encompasses: 'To me, sovereignty means having authority over one's life and culture. It is a right and something that should not have to be fought for. Terms such as self-determination are not high enough, not good enough terms for this' (Keown 2000: 62). Reflecting further on the terms that Grace chooses, I note the focus on 'authority', 'right', 'self-determination', terms which, as I discussed in Part One, are freighted by the specific histories, contexts, locations from which indigenous peoples speak. I remember too, that Larissa Behrendt argues that it is probably more useful, in an Australian context at least, to configure indigenous sovereignty together with 'self-determination', as embodying 'a list of claims or a series of tools' (2003: 106) through which indigenous communities negotiate their positioning and their aspirations in contemporary Australia (Part One). Notably, Behrendt places self-determination *with* sovereignty and the vocabulary of sovereignty that she offers is in many ways contiguous with the terms that striate Grace's delineation here, although, it is also clearly accented differently. One might say that sovereignty as Grace explicates it stands at one end of a continuum of power/authority at the other end of which lies powerlessness/subjugation. It is at once aligned with 'self-determination' as an analogous term but clearly distinguished from it. Here, self-determination might be understood broadly as the autonomy, authority and means to make decisions and choices about individual or communal cultural, material or spiritual resources informed by the genealogies of knowledge, law and story transmitted across generations.

In Grace's account, sovereignty is something that clearly precedes self-determination but that can be denied by the intervention of others in its practice. Its proper home or origin, it is implied, is in the domain of a right that should be inalienable, and not a site of struggle, not 'fought for'. But, importantly, in Grace's formulation, sovereignty is also personal, subjective and mobile. By framing her statement with the terms, 'to me', which implies and recognizes a range of other possible, overlapping, contrasting and indeed competing definitions, sovereignty is also, she implies, malleable. It is also *relational*. Indigenous sovereignty like the wider category of indigeneity, of which it is an important expression or component, takes shape with and against the definitions provided by others. It is allied with individual authority but extends into the domain of culture (which is a product of community) and aligned with the notion of having the autonomy and power to determine one's own modes of cultural engagement and expression. In recognizing these different but allied configurations of indigenous sovereignty (between Grace and Behrendt) we acknowledge that discourses of sovereignty and of indigeneity are often *shared* but also *specific*. As a key term through which indigenous peoples express their formal and informal claims to place, land and culture and by which they articulate the distinct values of their law, knowledges and histories, indigenous expressions of sovereignty often illustrate how indigeneity is embodied and realized in the everyday even as it is often denied in formal regimes of power.

SOVEREIGNTY, STORY, LAND

Sovereignty is often embodied and archived in 'story', for story conjoins physical spaces to mind as evidenced in Patricia Grace's mobilization of Māori *whakapapa* (genealogy) in *Dogside Story* as a dynamic, mobile archive of (emplaced) story articulating the foundations, precedents and coordinates of Māori law sustaining the life of the *whānau* (Part Two). Land and attachments to land are central to the unfolding of the story of sovereignty in Grace's work as in the work of other writers exploring the ways in which indigeneity is 'rooted in and routed through particular places' (Clifford 2006: 180). In its material, cultural and spiritual dimensions land and attachments to it (including diasporic ones), are a key marker of indigenous place.

We are of the land. It is our mother, *Papatuanuku*, our life sustainer. We need her. She doesn't need us though she was part of the plan which created our human-ness so that we could take care of her. She is the primary source of our cultural identity and our spiritual being. (Rika-Heke 1997: 174)

Powhiri Rika-Heke's dramatization of the place of land in Māori ontology emphasizes land as the site of the intersubstantiation of people and place (see Part One) and as a reciprocal relationship creating a set of self-defining duties of care as *tangata whenua* ('people of the land'). This idea is variously addressed and embodied in Patricia Grace's *Dogside Story* but is perhaps most obvious in the interweaving of Rua's assumption of his responsibilities for his daughter, Kid, with his learning to share the burden of cultural responsibilities, including those he assumes from his uncle on behalf of the community. Those cultural responsibilities are represented in part by his fishing, a form of provision and sustenance with its own paradigms and rules (what to reap from the seabed and what not to, where to fish and where not) that are contiguous with the forms of reciprocity or philosophy of care articulated by Rika-Heke above. Indeed, Clare Barker suggests that the defining moment of Rua's 'reintegration into his community' is in his 'assumption of a reciprocal role as both receiver of care and as a care*giver*' (Barker 2008: 130), further amplifying the (potentially) holistic role of responsibilities to land in indigenous imaginaries. This notion of responsibility is one that is also shared if differently accented across indigenous articulations and performance of the relationship between land and place. So, the Australian writer, Mudrooroo asserts, for example, that the character of indigenous ownership is 'not about possession in material terms' (although the struggle for material possession is long and ongoing), but should be understood rather as 'a responsibility held in sacred trust' (1995: 200) Here, Mudrooroo distinguishes Aboriginal configurations of ownership (as a set of cultural or spiritual responsibilities to place or 'country') from reigning configurations of land as a marker of economic possession in non-indigenous accounts of ownership. Historically, such accentuations of the role of land (as cultural and spiritual resource) in indigenous epistemologies (ways of knowing) have often been mobilized by non-indigenous as a way of diminishing such forms of ownership, often by emphasizing the nomadism of indigenous and/or ignoring evidence of forms of customary care to justify the expropriation of land. Andrew McGahan's *The White Earth* documents the prevalence of such moves in the histories of pastoral settlement, in the figuration of John McIvor and the corrosive effects of his enduring obsession with the idea of a singular, pure, absolute possession that is actively complicit in the obliteration of the physical and cultural remains and enduring claims of indigenous possession. While McIvor recognizes histories of Aboriginal occupation, McGahan illustrates how such forms of ownership can only be recognized by McIvor as such, in the terms provided by the defining 'logic of elimination' (Wolfe) organizing settler imaginings of place. That logic which promises the disappearance of the indigene, situates indigenous possession as always already becoming a thing of the past, thus confirming, in the process, the legitimacy, and as McIvor sees it in *The White Earth*, the superiority of settler forms of possession (always rendered in terms of economic success and sustainability).

In the aftermaths of colonial rule and the unmasking of its evacuations of indigenous place, to secure its own legitimacy, the repeal of the legal fiction of 'terra nullius' (under Mabo) in McGahan's Australia provides a foundational moment for the recuperation and reassertion of the cultural and spiritual as well as the material resources of 'country'. As Irene Watson argues, even as continuing state denial of indigenous sovereignty promotes the disconnection of

Aboriginal laws as Aboriginal peoples from country, 'continuing connections to country' are carved out 'from a place inside the "sovereign" space of the state, a space that guarantees no power to determine law-full obligations to country' (2009a, abstract). Such moves amplify the continuing forms of circumvention as of survival animating indigenous conceptions of sovereignty in national and transnational spaces.

CHAPTER FIVE

AFTERLIVES AND ADAPTATIONS

POSTCOLONIAL CINEMAS

African film – spotlight on Senegal

Senegal is one of an increasing number of African nations with a now substantial, vibrant and diverse body of cinematic representation and its most well known progenitor, Ousmane Sembene, played a critical role in the development of a distinctly postcolonial African cinema. While many African writers have established a tradition of working in a variety of genres and languages precisely in order to communicate with diverse audiences, including Ngũgĩ and Tsitsi Dangerembga, Sembene has moved between film and literature continuously. Establishing his reputation with novels like *Les Bouts de bois de Dieu* (*God's Bits of Wood*) (1960), an influential portrait of resistance that is too, according to David Murphy, 'a dazzling attempt to imagine a socialist future for the continent' (2007: 55), Sembene went on to direct at least twelve films as well as sustaining a prolific writing career. A number of his films are adaptations of his fiction and many broke new ground; Sembene was the first African filmmaker to make a film in an African language. *Mandabi* (*The Money Order*) (1968) was made in Wolof, the main language of Senegal. Notable among his other films are *La Noire De* (*Blackgirl*) (1966), *Xala* (1974), *Ceddo* (1977) *Faat Kiné* (2000), *Moolaadé* (*Protection*) (2004). Inspired by his Marxist commitments and influenced by the traditions of the West African *griot* (praise singers and storytellers), Sembene's films address questions of marginalization and exploitation; they expose the injustices and corruptions of the new African elites as well as those inherent in the old colonial order and direct particular attention too, to the lives of women. In *Xala*, for example, the oppressions of Africa's post-independence leaders are mirrored in the domestic abuses perpetrated by the film's family patriarch. This concern with women's realities and how they are shaped by overlapping structures of oppression (colonial and African) is revisited in his last films, *Faat Kiné* and *Moolaadé* (filmed and set in Burkino Faso), which, by and large, celebrate female resourcefulness and resistance, that 'heroism in daily life' Sembene sees as the abiding subject of his final trilogy (the last of which remains unfinished). In short, Sembene's films offer a distinctive portrait of African women's agency, while teasing out the contradictions and nuances of those extant social orders and traditions in which women actively intervene.

Safi Faye is a pioneering female film director and ethnographer whose films offer another lens through which to view the histories of Sub-Saharan African women, particularly those in rural areas. In films like *Kaddu Beykat* (*Letter from My Village*) (1975), *Fad'jal* (*Come and Work*) (1979), *Selbe et tant des autres* (*Selbe, One Among Many*) (1983) and *Mossane* (1996), which Faye describes as 'a song of women' (Pfaff 2004: 196), she chronicles the challenges facing rural women while celebrating their rituals, routines and interrelationships. In doing so, she foregrounds and challenges the extant histories and strategies of ethnographic film-making, often charged with objectifying and silencing its subjects. She facilitates instead the self-representation of African women, notably in *Selbe* (Foster 2005: 180). Her experimentalism is shared differently by the recently deceased, Djibril Diop Mambety, whose films, *Touki-Bouki* (1973), *Hyénes* (1992), *Le Franc* (1995), mix European film and dramatic traditions (allegory, surrealism) with African images and perspectives, to explore immigration, alienation, and globalization, critiquing particularly, the neocolonizing operations of the World Bank (*Hyénes*), a theme taken up too by the Malian director, Abderralima Sissako, in the perhaps more well known, if equally complex, *Bamako* (2006).

Film, Colonialism, Algeria

A number of important and provocative films directed by Europeans explore the passage of French colonialism in North Africa, particularly the bitter war of Independence with Algeria, and its complex contemporary legacies. Notable here is the work of the Italian neo-realist, Gillo Pontecorvo in *Battaglia di Algeri* (trans. *The Battle of Algiers*)

(1965) and of the Austrian, Michael Haneke whose *Caché* (*Hidden*) appeared in 2005, just a year after two other films excavating the question of Algeria and its place in France's 'memory wars': Alain Tasma's *Nuit Noire, October 17, 1961* and Philippe Faucon's *La Trahison* (*The Betrayal*). Faucon is also the director of two other engaging films, *Samia* (2000) and *Dans La Vie* (*In Life*) (2007) set among France's Middle Eastern and North African diasporas and exploring entrenched tensions in French society, connected to race, immigration and conditions of belonging. These tensions are memorably evinced too in Laurent Cantet's recent offering in a somewhat different genre, the classroom drama, in *Entre Les Murs* (*The Class*) (2009).

The Battle of Algiers is based on the memoirs of the film's Algerian producer, Saadi Youcef, imprisoned for his activities with the Algerian National Liberation Front (FLN), the liberation movement joined by Frantz Fanon and supported by Sembene. The film has been the subject of renewed critical attention in recent years particularly because of its attention to insurgency, histories of colonial occupation, biopolitics and discourses of sovereignty. Its re-emergence in wider critical accounts of cinema and post/colonialism comes after a period of some critical invisibility (particularly in France), often attributed to the controversial nature of its subject material. Recounting the events of a key year in the Algerian struggle against French occupation, the film offers an exploration of colonial violence and resistance, tracing the forms of action mobilized by Algeria's independence movement and the counter-insurgency tactics deployed by the French forces. It has generated a vast array of critical responses in and outside African locations. Among these, we might include the work of the prominent Algerian writer and director, Assia Djebar, centrally concerned with the greater picture of Arab women's histories in and outside African locations. While she is perhaps more well known in the Anglophone world for her collection of stories, *Femmes D'Alger dans leur apartment* (*Women of Algiers in Their Apartment*) (1980), the role of women in anti-colonial resistance is a key feature of her fictional portraits, particularly her Algerian quartet which opens with *L'Amour, La Fantasia* (*Fantasia: An Algerian Cavalcade*) (1985), and her films, *La Nouba des Femmes de Mont Chenoua* (1978) and *La Zerda ou les Chants de L'oubli* (*Zerda, or the Songs of Forgetfulness*) (1980). In her address of women's complex locations between feminism, nationalism and post/colonialism, she thus revisits and reworks a set of archives and images invoked but not fully developed in Pontecorvo's film.

Set for the most part, in the suburbs of Paris, and turning upon the consequences of secrets and lies, Michael Haneke's *Caché* (*Hidden*) is a compelling meditation on the unseen aftermaths of colonial trauma, guilt and complicity. At its centre, is the shaping influence of events that take place on 17 October 1961 in the aftermath of the violent suppression of popular demonstrations in Paris against French colonial policy in Algeria, which resulted in the death of between 50 and 200 protestors. Mirroring the brutalities of the war, this incident returns to haunt the contemporary moment and invade the private sphere (of the affluent urbanized Parisian middle classes), striking at the heart of its security and leaking doubt. Tracing the unlegislated (hidden) consequences of the intervention of one young boy in the adoption of another, recently orphaned, it invites us to probe the nature of complicity and the limits of responsibility, and makes striking, indeed, shocking use of suicide as a moral weapon, in seeming indictment of the collective as the individual for failures to adequately remember and care for those others marginalized and/ or brutalized within their domain. Given its very specific rooting in the historical context of French colonialism in Algeria, it might be seen as in dialogue with Pontecorvo's film and with contemporary cultural discussions of terror and terrorism focused on the import of variant forms of (suicide as) insurgency that increasingly mark diverse sites of conflict (Iraq, Afghanistan, Chechnya, Israel/Palestine, Sri Lanka) and whose origins are often locatable in longer standing colonial and postcolonial histories.

Adapting Aotearoa/New Zealand – indigeneity and film

A diverse body of contemporary New Zealand films, indigenous and non-indigenous, excavates the charged and often traumatic histories of colonialism while offering a distinctive lens on New Zealand identities. The work of Jane Campion, one of New Zealand's most exciting directors, now resident in Australia, illustrates some of the useful questions that we might ask of the forms of adaptation at work in postcolonial cultural production (across a range of genres), given that literary adaptation and biopic figure highly in her work. Having just released *Bright Star* (2009), based on the romance between the Romantic poet John Keats and Fanny Brawne, Campion recently acquired the film rights to the short story, 'Runaway', by Canadian author, Alice Munro, which is to be her next film project. She made her international name with films like *Sweetie* (1989) and *An Angel at My Table*, the latter based on the autobiographies of an exciting New Zealand writer, Janet Frame. The first New Zealander (and the first woman) to earn a Palme d'Or at Cannes with *The Piano* (1993), Campion also subsequently co-authored a novelization of the film, with Kate Pullinger, entitled *The Piano: A Novel* (1994). While *The Piano* has occasionally been linked by some of its viewers with an earlier novel by another New Zealander, Jane Mander's *The Story of a New Zealand River* (1920), its complex literary genealogy doesn't stop there. Campion, as Ken Gelder (1999) observes, has invited us to consider the film as inspired by her love of Emily Brontë's classic novel, *Wuthering Heights* (1847), a move which also invites us to revisit the relationships between the canon of English literature and postcolonial cultural production more generally. In Part One, I explored the tradition within postcolonial writing of responding to the canon and the forms of cultural authority with which it is imbued. One might ask, in turn, how useful it is to consider Campion's film in this light. How does it engage with or interrogate the values and ideologies of its canonical antecedent? How does it re-site and recite *Wuthering Heights*? In revisiting the troubled terrain of early colonial history and the genre of (colonial) romance to amplify the dislocations and dispossessions of settlement, we might also ask how far the film reinstates the romance genre's reliance on what Terrie Goldie has termed, the 'standard commodities' (viz. sex, violence, orality, the prehistoric, mysticism) constituting the 'semiotic field of the indigene' (1989)?

Indigeneity is a central concern too, albeit from different locations, of a range of other recent films. The work of the Māori writers, Alan Duff and Witi Ihimaera has produced a range of interesting adaptations, including Leo Tamahori's *Once Were Warriors* (1994) and Ian Mune's *What Becomes of the Broken Hearted?* (1999). Both trace the lives of contemporary Māori but the manner in which they do so has often been a source of critical discussion. The novelist (Alan Duff), on whom both of these films rely for their underlying plot, characters and focus, has been alternately praised and criticized for his representation of marginalized urban Māori communities set on a path of destruction from within. While both adaptations, like Duff's novel work to draw attention to questions of social inequality and exclusion, Tamahori's adaptation of Duff's novel has been charged with failing to adequately reflect the social, economic and political contexts that lie behind the forms of enfranchisement and disenfranchisement characterizing Māori communities in the novel. It is thus also often seen by critics as promulgating negative stereotypes, of 'providing graphic violence at the expense of social analysis' (Thornley 2001: 28). Wider questions concerning the histories of indigenous representation and ownership of story together with larger debates about the nature of cultural appropriation are also critical to an engagement with Niki Caro's internationally successful film, *Whale Rider* (2002). Adapted from a Witi Ihimaera novella (*The Whale Rider*, 1987) and produced in dialogue with the 'Ngati Porou' people of Whangara (where the film is set), *Whale Rider* delineates the story of a young girl, Pai, seeking to redefine her place in her community. The film tracks her battles to gain the trust and assurance of her grandfather in proving that she is fit to lead, a position eventually secured, Ann Hardy suggests, by her seemingly telepathic connection with a *taniwha* (figure of Māori spirituality) in the form of a whale (2003). If Pai's journey suggests, as some have argued, something of how indigenous myth can be mobilized as a dynamic resource in acts of decolonization, it also raises interesting and rather more problematic questions about the ways in which cultural and spiritual resources are often adapted, transformed and/or exploited in catering for the needs and desires of *Pakeha* and/or global non-indigenous (Huggan 2001, Hardy 2003).

Story, as I've noted earlier, plays a pivotal role in indigenous conceptions of sovereignty. One of the many debates fired by the appearance of *Whalerider*, as many critics have noted, was a renewed attention in Aotearoa/New Zealand to questions of cultural ownership and appropriation, not least, among indigenous film-makers. At least one of those who articulated his disquiet with the ways in which *Whalerider* was promoted was Barry Barclay, the Maori film-maker and theorist, who coined the term, 'Fourth cinema', to encapsulate his ideas of what an 'Indigenous Cinema with a capital "I"' (2003: 7) might look like. In doing so, he sought to produce a distinctly accented theorization of its place in relation to the extant framework of First, Second and Third cinemas (denoting Hollywood, arthouse and third world film respectively). Barclay's wider investment in indigenous issues over a long career generated a distinctive method and philosophy of film-making which emphasizes, as Stuart Murray has argued, 'community inclusion and a reciprocity between the film-maker and the filmed as well as the necessary modification of classical film techniques in the telling of Maori stories' (2007: 89). Barclay's feature films like *Ngati* (1987) and *Te Rua* (1991), in their form as their content, give flesh to these overarching concerns with the key principles of Māori sovereignty, that also inform Patricia Grace's *Dogside Story* (Part Two and above). Barclay's methods are increasingly reflected in diverse forms of collaboration between indigenous writers, directors and local communities in a range of new films that explicitly address dialogues within and between indigenous about the fabric of Māori futures. Armagan Ballantyne's *The Strength of Water* (2009) and Shane Loader and Andrea Bosshard's *Taking the Waewae Express* (2008) are instructive recent examples.

READING

Colonialism, psychoanalysis, postcolonialisms

- Anthony Elliott, *Psychoanalytic Theory: An Introduction* (2002)
- Robert Young, *White Mythologies, Writing History and the West* (1990)
- Ranjana Khanna, *Dark Continents: Psychoanalysis and Colonialism* (2003)
- Jennifer Rutherford, *The Gauche Intruder: Freud, Lacan and the White Australian Fantasy* (2001)
- Jacques Derrida, *The Postcard: From Socrates to Freud and Beyond* (1980), *Archive Fever: A Freudian Impression* (1995)
- Jacques Derrida (author), Peggy Kamuf and Elizabeth Rottenberg (eds), *Psyche: Inventions of the Other* Vol. 1 (2007), Vol. 2 (2008)
- Nicholas Abram and Maria Torok, *The Wolfman's Magic Word: A Cryptonomy* (1976)
- Sloan Mahone and Megan Vaughan, (eds), *Psychiatry and Empire* (2007)
- Gillian Whitlock and Kate Douglas, (eds), *Trauma Texts* (2009)
- Peter Buse and Andrew Stott, (eds), *Ghosts, Deconstruction, Psychoanalysis* (1999)
- Dominick LaCapra, *Writing History, Writing Trauma* (2001)

Postcolonial cinema

- Felicity Collins and Therese Davis (2004), *Australian Cinema after Mabo*. (Victoria: Melbourne University Press)
- Frank Ukadike and Teshome H. Gabriel (eds) (2002), *Questioning African Cinema*. (Minneapolis: University of Minnesota Press)
- David Murphy and Patrick Williams (2007), *Postcolonial African Cinema: Ten Directors* (Manchester: University of Manchester Press) Nurith Gertz and George Khleifi, *Palestinian Cinema: Landscape, Trauma and Memory* (2008)
- Ian Conrich and Stuart Murray, *New Zealand Filmmakers* (2007)
- Vijay Mishra, *Bollywood Cinema – Temples of Desire* (2002)

RESEARCH

- Identify some common characteristics of a psychoanalytic approach to reading texts. What does a psychoanalytic reading aim to explore? What key people, terms and ideas would you need to engage with in order to further understand the components of such an approach?
- What do you understand by terms like 'Other', trauma, memory, displacement, neurosis, mourning, fantasy, taboo? Do some research to discover the relevance and meaning of these terms for psychoanalytic theory and psychoanalytic approaches.
- What do you understand by the term 'hybridity'? Identify some of the ways in which it is used in developing understandings of postcolonial literatures and cultures.
- Locate two or more theorists (e.g. Homi K. Bhabha, Stuart Hall, Robert Young) for whom hybridity is a key site of discussion. Pick one of their texts (e.g. *The Location of Culture*) and establish some key points of debate in their discussion of hybridities.
- Consider the critical accounts of the 'border' offered in a select range of postcolonial cultural production and theory of your choice. What social, cultural or political implications accrue around the border?
- Compare and contrast the ways in which island or land locked states imagine their borders in literature? How are the borders between continents imagined or traversed in postcolonial literatures? How are Europe's borders imagined in postcolonial cultural production?

Extended research topic

Combine an examination of representations of the border in the cultural production of partitioned states (India–Palestine, Ireland, India–Pakistan) with a delineation of the critical ideas that pertain to 'borders' in the work of a number of theorists.
Or
How important are the notion of borders in indigenous literatures and theory? What resonances accrue around 'borders' in indigenous representations of identity? How do such visions connect with or depart from the 'border' as a figure in diasporic writing?

Note: This also involves researching the connections within and between indigenous and diasporic literatures and cultures as many indigenous live in diaspora (Māori in Australia, First Nations in the US).

BIBLIOGRAPHY

Achebe, Chinua. (1997), 'An Image of Africa: Racism in Conrad's *Heart of Darkness*' in Bart Moore-Gilbert, et al. (eds), *Postcolonial Criticism*. London and New York: Longman.

—(2006), 'Named for Victoria, Queen of England' in Bill Ashcroft et al. (eds), *The Postcolonial Studies Reader* (Second Edition). London: Routledge, pp. 143–5.

Adichie, Chimamanda Ngozi. (2005), *Purple Hibiscus*. London: Harper Perennial.

Ahluwalia, Pal. (2006), 'Négritude and Nativism' in B. Ashcroft et al. (eds), *The Post-Colonial Studies Reader* (Second Edition). London and New York: Routledge, pp. 230–3.

Ahmad, Aijaz. (1992), *In Theory: Classes, Nations, Literatures*. London: Verso.

Ali, Monica. (2003), *Brick Lane*. London and New York: Doubleday.

Allen, Chadwick. (2002), *Blood Narrative: Indigenous Identity in American Indian and Maori Literary and Activist Texts*. Durham, NC: Duke University Press.

Allon, Fiona. (2002), 'Boundary Anxieties: Between Borders and Belongings' (38 paras), *Borderlands ejournal* 1, (2). Available: http://www.borderlands. net.au/vol1no2_2002/allon_boundary.html

Ang, Ien. (2001), *On Not Speaking Chinese: Living between Asia and the West*. London: Routledge.

Anzaldúa, Gloria. (1987), *Borderlands/La Frontera: The New Mestiza*. San Francisco, CA: Aunt Lute Books.

Ashcroft, Bill, Griffiths, Gareth, and Tiffin, Helen. (eds) (2006), *The Post-Colonial Studies Reader* (Second Edition). London and New York: Routledge.

Attwood, Bain and Forster, S.G. (eds) (2003), *Frontier Conflict: The Australian Experience*. Canberra: National Museum of Australia.

Bakhtin, Mikhail. (1984), *Rabelais and His World*. Trans. by Hélène Iswolsky. Bloomington, IN: Indiana University Press.

Ballantyne, Armagnan. (Dir.) (2009), *The Strength of Water*. New Zealand and Germany: Hopscotch Films.

Barclay, Barry. (2003), 'Celebrating Fourth Cinema', *Illusions* 35: 7–12.

Barghouti, Mourid. (2004), *I Saw Ramallah*. Trans. by Ahdaf Soueif. London: Bloomsbury.

Barker, Clare. (2008), '"Bionic *Waewae*" and "Iron Crutches": *Turangawaewae,* Disability, and Prosthesis in Patricia Grace's *Dogside Story*', *Moving Worlds* 8, (2): 120–33.

Behrendt, Larissa. (2003), *Achieving Social Justice – Indigenous Rights and Australia's Future.* Sydney: The Federation Press.

Bernard, Anna. (2007), '"Who would Dare to Make it into an Abstraction": Mourid Barghouti's *I Saw Ramallah*', *Textual Practice* 21, (4): 665–86.

Bhabha, Homi. K. (ed.) (1990), *Nation and Narration.* London: Routledge.

—(1994), *The Location of Culture.* London: Routledge.

Bird Rose, Deborah. (2004), *Reports from a Wild Country: Ethics for Decolonisation.* Sydney: University of New South Wales Press.

Boehmer, Elleke. (2002), *Empire, the National and the Postcolonial 1890–1920: Resistance in Interaction.* Oxford and New York: Oxford University Press.

—(2005), *Stories of Women: Gender and Narrative in the Postcolonial Nation.* Manchester: Manchester University Press, 2005.

Boland, Eavan. (1995), *Object Lessons: The life of the woman and the poet in our time.* Manchester: Carcanet, 1995.

Brah, Avtar. (1996), *Cartographies of Diaspora: Contesting Identities.* London: Routledge.

Brah, Avtar, and Annie. E. Coombs. (eds) (2000), *Hybridity and Its Discontents: Politics, Science, Culture.* London: Routledge.

Brewster, Anne. (1996), *Aboriginal Women's Autobiography.* Sydney: Oxford University Press/Sydney University Press.

—(2005), 'Remembering Whiteness: Reading Indigenous Life Narrative' (38 paras), *Borderlands ejournal* 4, (1). Available: http://www.borderlands. net.au/vol4no1_2005/brewster_remembering.htm

Bulhan, Hussein Abdilahi. (1985), *Frantz Fanon and the Psychology of Oppression.* New York: Plenum Press.

Burke, Anthony. (2002), 'The Perverse Perseverance of Sovereignty' (66 paras), *Borderlands ejournal* 1, (2). Available: http://www.borderlands.net.au/ vol1no2_2002/burke_perverse.html

Campion, Jane. (Dir.) (1993), *The Piano.* NSW Film and Television Office, Jan Chapman Productions, CIBY 2000, Australian Film Commission.

Caro, Niki. (Dir.) (2002), *Whale Rider.* New Zealand: South Pacific Pictures Ltd.

Carter, Paul. (1987), *The Road to Botany Bay: An Essay in Spatial History.* London: Faber & Faber.

—(1996), *The Lie of the Land.* London: Faber & Faber.

Chambers, Iain. (2001), *Culture after Humanism: History, Culture, Subjectivity.* London and New York: Routledge.

Chaudhuri, Amit. (2001), *Three Novels: A Strange and Sublime Address, Afternoon Raag, Freedom Song.* London. Picador.

Cheah, Pheng. (2003), *Spectral Nationality: Passages of Freedom from Kant to Postcolonial Literatures of Liberation.* New York: Columbia University Press.

Cleary, Joseph. (2002), *Literature, Partition and the Nation State: Culture and Conflict in Ireland, Israel and Palestine.* Cambridge: Cambridge University Press.

Clifford, James. (2006), 'Indigenous Articulations' in B. Ashcroft et al. (eds), *The Post-Colonial Studies Reader* (Second Edition). London: Routledge, pp. 180–3.

Cobo, José R. Martinez. (1986), *Study on the Problem of Discrimination Against Indigenous Populations*, UN Doc.E/CN.4/Sub.2/1986/7 and Add.1–4.

Cohen, Robin. (2008), *Global Diasporas – An Introduction* (Second Edition [first edition, 1997]). London and New York: Routledge.

Damm, Kateri. (1993), 'Says Who: Colonialism, Identity and Defining Indigenous Literature' in Jeanette Armstrong (ed.), *Looking at the Words of Our People: First Nations Analysis of Literature*. Penticton, British Columbia: Theytus Books.

Dangor, Achmat. (2004), 'Another Country', *The Guardian Review*, 25 September: 37.

David, Murphy and Williams, Patrick. (2007), *Postcolonial African Cinema: Ten Directors*. Manchester: Manchester University Press.

Davis, Therese. (2007), 'Remembering our Ancestors: Cross-cultural Collaboration and the Mediation of Aboriginal Culture and History in *Ten Canoes* (Rolf de Heer, 2006)', *Studies in Australasian Cinema* 1, (1): 5–15.

De Kock, Leon, Bethlehem, L. and Laden, S. (eds) (2004), *South Africa in the Global Imaginary*. Pretoria: University of South Africa Press.

Derrida, Jacques. (1998), *Archive Fever: A Freudian Impression*. Trans. by Eric Prenowitz. Chicago, IL: University of Chicago Press.

Diedrich, Maria, Gates Jr., H. and Pedersen, C. (eds) (1999), *Black Imagination and the Middle Passage*. New York and Oxford: Oxford University Press.

Dirk Moses, A. (ed.) (2008), *Empire, Colony, Genocide*. New York: Berghahn Books.

Dirlik, Arif. (1994), 'The Postcolonial Aura: Third World Criticism in the Age of Global Capitalism', *Critical Inquiry* 20: 328–56.

Durrant, Sam. (2005), 'The Invention of Mourning in Post-Apartheid Literature', *Third World Quarterly* 26, (3): 441–50.

Eagleton, Terry. (1995), *Heathcliff and the Great Hunger: Studies in Irish Culture*. London: Verso.

Eakin, Paul John. (1999), *How Our Lives Become Stories: Making Selves*. Ithaca, NY: Cornell University Press.

Eisenstein, Zillah. (2000), 'Writing Bodies on the Nation for the Globe' in S. Ramchod-Nilsson and M.A. Tétreault (eds), *Women, States and Nationalism: At Home in the Nation?* London: Routledge, pp. 35–53.

Evans, Julie. (2008), 'Beyond the Pale: Sovereignty, Legitimacy and Indigenous Peoples'. Unpublished paper presented at the Menzies Centre for Australian Studies, King's College London, 5 November.

Fanon, Frantz. (1986), *Black Skins, White Masks* Trans. Charles Lam Markmann. New York: Grove Press Inc. [Revised edition, originally translated and published in English 1967].

Faye, Safi. (Dir.) (1996), *Mossane*. Senegal: Muss Cinématographie.

Fee, Margery. (2006), 'Who Can Write As Other?' in B. Ashcroft et al. (eds), *The Post-Colonial Studies Reader* (Second Edition). London: Routledge, pp. 169–71.

Foster, Gwendolyn Audrey. (2005), 'Safi Faye and Trinh T. Minh-ha' in J. Petrolle and V. Wright Wexman (eds), *Women and Experimental Filmmaking*. Chicago, IL: University of Illinois Press, pp. 177–93.

Gelder, Ken. (1999), 'Jane Campion and the Limits of Literary Cinema' in D. Cartmell and I. Whelehan (eds), *Adaptations – From Text to Screen, Screen to Text*. London: Routledge, pp. 157–72.

Gelder, Ken and Jane M. Jacobs. (1998), *Uncanny Australia: Sacredness and Identity in a Postcolonial Nation*. Melbourne: Melbourne University Press.

Gilroy, Paul. (1993), *The Black Atlantic: Modernity and Double Consciousness*. London: Verso.

Goldie, Terry. (1989), *Fear and Temptation – The Image of the Indigene in Canadian, Australian and New Zealand Literatures*. Montreal and Kingston: McGill-Queen's University Press.

Grace, Patricia. (2001), *Dogside Story*. London: The Women's Press.

Gramsci, Antonio. (1971), *Prison Notebooks*. Trans. Quintin Hoare and Geoffrey Novell-Smith. New York: International Publishers.

Grenville, Kate. (2005), *The Secret River*. Edinburgh: Canongate Books.

—(2007), *Searching for the Secret River*. Edinburgh: Canongate Books.

Griffiths, Gareth. (1994), 'The Myth of Authenticity: representation, discourse and social practice' in Chris Tiffin and Alan Lawson, eds, *De-scribing Empire: post-coloniality and textuality*. London: Routledge, pp. 70–85.

Griswold, Wendy. (2000), *Bearing Witness: Readers, Writers, and the Novel in Nigeria*. New Jersey: Princeton University Press.

Hall, Stephen. (1992), *Mapping the Next Millennium*. New York: Random House.

Hall, Stuart. (1994), 'Cultural Identity and Diaspora' in P. Williams and L.Chrisman (eds), *Colonial Discourse and Post-colonial Theory: A Reader*. Edinburgh and Essex: Pearson Education, pp. 392–403.

Haneke, Michael. (Dir.) (2005), *Caché (Hidden)*. Austria and Germany: Artificial Eye.

Hardy, Ann. (2003/4), 'Return of the Taniwha: The Re-Spiritualization of Land and Film in Aotearoa', *British Review of New Zealand Studies* 14: 87–104.

Harley, J.B. (1992), 'Deconstructing the Map' in Trevor Barnes and James Duncan (eds), *Writing Worlds*. London: Routledge, pp. 231–47.

Haverty-Rugg, Linda. (1997), *Picturing Ourselves: Photography and Autobiography*. Chicago, IL: University of Chicago Press.

Hiddleston, Jane. (2005), 'Shapes and Shadows: (Un) veiling the Immigrant in Monica Ali's *Brick Lane*', *Journal of Commonwealth Literature* 40, (1): 57–72.

Hochberg, Gil. Z. (2006), 'Edward Said: "The Last Jewish Intellectual" On Identity, Alterity, and the Politics of Memory', *Social Text* 87, 24 (2): 47–65.

Howe, Stephen. (2002), *Empire: A Very Short Introduction*. Oxford: Oxford University Press.

Hoy, Helen. (2001), *How Should I Read These? Native Women Writers in Canada*. Toronto: University of Toronto Press.

Huddart, David. (2006), *Homi Bhabha*. London: Routledge.

Huggan, Graham. (1994), *Territorial Disputes: Maps and Mapping Strategies in Canadian and Australian Fiction*. Toronto: University of Toronto Press.

—(2001), *The Postcolonial Exotic: Marketing the Margins*. London: Routledge.

—(2007), *Australian Literature – Postcolonialism, Racism, Transnationalism*. Oxford: Oxford University Press.

Huggan, Graham and Tiffin, Helen. (2007), 'Green Postcolonialisms', *Interventions* 9, (1), 1–11.

Huggins, Jackie. (2003), 'Always Was Always Will Be' in Michele Grossman (ed.), *Blacklines: Contemporary Critical Writing by Indigenous Australians*. Carlton Victoria: Melbourne University Press, pp. 60–6.

Hulme, Peter. (1986), *Colonial Encounters: Europe and the Native Caribbean 1492–1797*. London: Methuen.

Hutcheon, Linda. (1988), *A Poetics of Postmodernism: History, Theory, Fiction*. London and New York: Routledge.

—(1991), *Splitting Images: Contemporary Canadian Ironies*. Oxford: Oxford University Press.

Ihimaera, Witi and Peter Mares. (2009), 'Revisiting Fiction with Witi Ihimaera', *The Book Show* ABC Radio National, 5 May 2009. Accessed 7 May 2009 at http://www.abc.net.au/rn/bookshow/stories/2009/2558016.htm

Jaggi, Maya. (1994), 'Crossing The River – Caryl Phillips Talks to Maya Jaggi', *Wasafiri* 20: 25–30.

—(2001), 'Caryl Phillips', *The Guardian Review*. Saturday 3 November: 6–7.

Jameson, Fredric. (1986), 'Third-world Literature in the Era of Multinational capitalism', *Social Text* 15: 65–88.

Kabir, Ananya. (2009), *Territory of Desire: Representing the Valley of Kashmir*. Minneapolis, MN: University of Minnesota Press.

Katrak, Ketu H. (1992), 'Indian Nationalism, Gandhian "Satyagraha" and Representations of Female Sexuality' in A. Parker, M. Russo, D. Sommer and P. Yaeger (eds), *Nationalisms & Sexualities*. London: Routledge, pp. 395–406.

Keown, Michelle. (2000) 'Interview with Patricia Grace', *Kunapipi*, 22, (2): 54–63.

—(2005), *Postcolonial Pacific Writing*. London: Routledge.

Lazarus, Neil. (2004), 'Fredric Jameson on "Third-World Literature": A Qualified Defence' in D.Kellner and S. Homer (eds), *Fredric Jameson: A Critical Reader*. Basingstoke: Palgrave Macmillan, pp. 42–62.

Lindholm Schulz, Helena. (2003), *The Palestinian Diaspora: Formations of Identity and Politics of Homeland*. London: Routledge.

Lloyd, David. (2005), 'The Indigent Sublime: Specters of Irish Hunger', *Representations* 92: 152–87.

Loomba, Ania. (1998), *Colonialism/Postcolonialism*. London: Routledge.

Low, Gail. (2006), 'The Natural Artist: Publishing Amos Tutuola's *The Palm Wine-Drinkard* in Post-War Britain', *Research in African Literatures* 37, (4): 15–33.

—(2009), *Publishing the Postcolonial: West African and Caribbean Writing in the UK, 1950–1967*. London: Routledge.

Mabura, Lily G.N. (2008), 'Breaking Gods: An African Postcolonial Gothic Reading of Chimamanda Ngozi Adichie's *Purple Hibiscus* and *Half of a Yellow Sun*', *Research in African Literatures* 39, (1): 203–22.

Mason, Victoria. (2007), 'Children of the "Idea of Palestine": Negotiating Identity, Belonging and Homeland in the Palestinian Diaspora', *Journal of Intercultural Studies* 28, (3): 271–85.

Mbembé, Achille. (2001), *On the Postcolony*. Berkeley, CA: University of California Press.

Mbembe, Achille, and Nuttall, Sarah. (2004), 'Writing the World from an African Metropolis', *Public Culture* 16, (3): 347–72.

McGahan, Andrew. (2004), *The White Earth*. New York: Soho Press.

McGonegal, Julie. (2005), 'Postcolonial Metacritique – Jameson, Allegory and the Always – Already-Read Third World Text', *Interventions* 7, (2): 251–65.

McKenna, Mark. (2004), *This Country: A Reconciled Republic?* Sydney, NSW: University of New South Wales Press.

McLean, Ian. (1998), *White Aborigines: Identity Politics in Australian Art*. Cambridge: Cambridge University Press.

McLeod, John. (2004), *Postcolonial London: Rewriting the Metropolis*. London: Routledge.

Mills, Sara. (1993), *Discourses of Difference: An Analysis of Women's Travel Writing and Colonialism*. London:Routledge.

Mishra, Vijay. (2002), *Bollywood Cinema – Temples of Desire*. London: Routledge.

—(2007), *The Literature of the Indian Diaspora – Theorizing the Diasporic Imaginary*. Abingdon, Oxon and New York: Routledge.

Mohanty, Chandra. (1984), 'Under Western Eyes: Feminist Scholarship and Colonial Discourses', *Feminist Review* 30: 65–88.

Mohanty, Chandra Talpade. (2003), *Feminism Without Borders: Decolonizing Theory, Practising Solidarity*. Durham, NC: Duke University Press.

Moore-Gilbert, Bart, Stanton, Gareth and Maley, Willy. (eds) (1997), *Postcolonial Criticism*. London and New York: Longman.

Moreton-Robinson, Aileen. (2000), *Talkin' Up to the White Woman: Indigenous Women and Feminism*. St Lucia: University of Queensland Press.

—(2003), "I Still Call Australia Home": Indigenous Belonging and Place in a white Postcolonising Society' in S. Ahmed et al., *Uprootings/Regroundings: Postcoloniality, Home and Place*. London and New York: Berg, pp. 23–40.

—(ed.) (2007), *Sovereign Subjects – Indigenous Sovereignty Matters*. Crows Nest, NSW: Allen & Unwin.

Mudrooroo. (1995), *Us Mob: History, Culture, Struggle: An Introduction to Aboriginal Australia*. Sydney: Angus & Robertson.

Mullan, John. (2004), 'Foreign Thoughts', *The Guardian Review*, 29 May 2004: 32.

Murray, Stuart. (2007), 'Images of Dignity, the Films of Barry Barclay' in Ian Conrich and Stuart Murray (eds), *New Zealand Filmmakers*. Michigan: Wayne State University Press, pp. 88–103.

Nicholls, Brendon and Murray, Stuart. (2008), 'Rethinking Indigeneity Research Network, Inaugural Workshop'. University of Leeds.

Nicoll, Fiona. (2002), 'De-facing *Terra Nullius* and Facing the Public Secret of Indigenous Sovereignty in Australia', (50 paras) *Borderlands ejournal* 1, (2). Available: http://www.borderlands.net.au/issues/vol1no2.html

Obama, Barack. (2008), *Dreams From My Father: A Story of Race and Inheritance*. Edinburgh: Canongate Books.

Orr, Bridget. (2006), 'The Maori House of Fiction' in D. Lynch and W.B. Warner (eds), *Cultural Institutions of the Novel*. Durham, NC: Duke University Press, pp.73–96.

Paradies, Yin C. (2006), 'Beyond Black and White: Essentialism, Hybridity and Indigeneity', *Journal of Sociology* 42, (4): 355–67.

Parry, Benita. (2004), *Postcolonial Studies: A Materialist Critique*. London: Routledge.

Pathe, Rajeev. S. (2001), 'Frantz Fanon', in J.C. Hawley (ed.), *Encyclopedia of Postcolonial Studies*. Santa Barbara, CA: Greenwood Press, pp. 162–7.

Patterson, Amy S. (2007), 'The New Globalization and HIV/AIDS in Africa' in George Klay Kieh (ed.), *Africa and the New Globalization*. London: Ashgate, pp. 155–77.

Paxman, Jeremy, 'Newsnight', BBC2, Broadcast, 5 November 2008.

Perfect, Michael. (2008), 'The Multicultural *Bildungsroman*: Stereotypes in *Brick Lane*', *Journal of Commonwealth Literature* 43, (3): 109–20.

Pfaff, Françoise. (2004), *Focus on African Films*. Bloomington, IN: Indiana University Press.

Pontecorvo, Gillo. (Dir.) (1965), *Battaglia di Algeri* (*The Battle of Algiers*). Algeria and Italy: Casbah Films.

Pratt, Mary Louise. (1992), *Imperial Eyes: Travel Writing and Transculturation*. London: Routledge.

Probyn-Rapsey, Fiona. (2007), 'Complicity, Critique and Methodology', *Ariel* 38, (2–3): 65–83.

Procter, J. (2003), *Dwelling Places: Postwar Black British Writing*. Manchester: Manchester University Press.

—(2006), 'The Postcolonial Everyday', *New Formations: A Journal of Culture/Theory/Politics* 58: 62–80.

—(2007), 'Diaspora', in J. McLeod (ed.), *The Routledge Companion to Postcolonial Studies*. New York: Routledge, pp. 151–9.

Quayson, Ato. (2000), *Postcolonialism: Theory, Practice or Process?* Oxford: Blackwell.

Rabinow, Paul. (1984), *The Foucault Reader*. London: Penguin.

Rika-Heke, Powhiri. (1997), 'Tribes or Nation? Post or Fence? What's the Matter with Self-Definition' in Stuart Murray (ed.), *Not on Any Map: Essays on Postcoloniality and Cultural Nationalism*. Exeter: University of Exeter Press, pp. 170–80.

Rose, Jacqueline. (2007), *The Last Resistance*. London: Verso Books.

Roy, Arundhati. (2001), *Power Politics*. Cambridge, MA: Southend Press.

Rushdie, Salman. (1995), *Shame* (1983). London: Vintage

—(2006), 'Imaginary Homelands', in B. Ashcroft et al. (eds), *The Post-Colonial Studies Reader* (Second Edition). London: Routledge, pp. 428–34.

Rushdie, Salman and Elizabeth West. (1997), *The Vintage Book of Indian Writing 1947–1997*. London: Vintage.

Ryan, Simon. (1996), *The Cartographic Eye: How Explorers Saw Australia*. Cambridge: Cambridge University Press.

Said, Edward. (1978), *Orientalism*. London: Routledge and Kegan Paul.

—(1983), *The World, the Text and the Critic*. Cambridge, MA: Harvard University Press.

—(1993), *Culture and Imperialism*. London: Chatto and Windus.

—(1999), *After the Last Sky*. (Second Edition) New York: Columbia University Press.

San Juan, Epifania. (1998), *Beyond Postcolonial Theory?* New York: St Martins Press.

Sembene, Ousmane. (1986), *God's Bits of Wood*. Trans. by Francis Price. London: Heinemann.

—(Dir.) (2000), *Faat Kiné*. Senegal: Filmi Domireew.

—(Dir.) (2004), *Moolaadé*. Senegal: Filmi Domireew.

Sharpe, Jenny. (2002), 'A Conversation with Gayatri Spivak: Politics and Imagination', *Signs: Journal of Women in Culture and Society* 28, (2): 609–24.

Shiva, Vandana. (2002), *Water Wars: Privatisation, Pollution and Profit*. London: Pluto Press.

Shohat, Ella. (1992), 'Notes on the "Post-Colonial"', *Social Text* 31/32: 99–113.

Smith, Sidonie and Schaffer, Kay. (2004), *Human Rights and Narrated Lives: The Ethics of Recognition*. New York: Palgrave Macmillan.

Somerville, Alice Te Punga. (2007), 'The Lingering War Captain: Maori Texts, Indigenous Contexts', *Journal of New Zealand Literature* 24, (2): 20–43.

Sorkin, Michael. (ed.) (2005), *Against the Wall – Israel's Barrier to Peace*. New York and London: The New Press.

Spivak, Gayatri. (1985), 'Three Women's Texts and a Critique of Imperialism', *Critical Inquiry* 12, (1): 243–61.

—(1988), 'Can the Subaltern Speak?' in C. Nelson and L.Grossberg (eds), *Marxism and the Interpretation of Cultures*. Urbana, IL: University of Illinois Press, pp. 271–313.

—(1999), *A Critique of Postcolonial Reason: Toward a History of theVanishing Present*. Cambridge, MA and London: Harvard University Press.

Stallybrass, Peter and White, Allon. (1986), *The Politics and Poetics of Transgression*. London: Methuen.

Stratton, Jon. (2004), 'Borderline Anxieties: What whitening the Irish has to do with Keeping Out Asylum Seekers' in Aileen Moreton-Robinson (ed.), *Whitening Race*. Canberra: Aboriginal Studies Press, pp. 222–39.

Tamahori, Lee. (Dir.) (1994), *Once Were Warriors*. New Zealand: Footprint films.

Thornley, Davinia. (2001), 'White, Brown, or "Coffee"? Revisioning Race in Lee Tamahori's *Once Were Warriors*', *Film Criticism* 25, (3): 22–36.

Triuizi, Alessandro. (1996), 'African Cities, Historical Memory and Street Buzz' in I. Chambers and L. Curti (eds), *The Post-Colonial Question: Common Skies, Divided Horizons*. London: Routledge, pp. 78–91.

Turner, Graeme. (1986), *National Fictions: Literature, Film and the Construction of Australian Narrative*. Sydney: Allen and Unwin.

Turner, Stephen. (2008), 'Compulsory Nationalism', *Moving Worlds* 8, (2): 7–27.

UNESCO. (2008), *Education for All: Global Monitoring Report – Regional Overview, Sub-Saharan Africa*. Available at www.efareport.unesco.org

Van der Vlies, Andrew. (2007), *South African Textual Cultures: White, Black, Read All Over*. Manchester: Manchester University Press.

Vasquez, Jose Santiago Fernandez. (2002), 'Recharting the Geography of Genre', *Journal of Commonwealth Literature* 37, (2): 85–106.

Veracini, Lorenzo. (2007), 'Historylessness: Australia as a Settler Colonial Collective', *Postcolonial Studies* 10, (3): 271–85.

—(2008), 'Colonialism and Genocides: Notes for an Analysis of the Settler Archive' in A. Dirk Moses (ed.), *Empire, Colony, Genocide*. New York and Oxford: Berghahn Books, pp. 148–62.

Verhoeven, Deb. (2009), *Jane Campion*. London: Routledge.

Walcott, Derek. (1998), *What the Twilight Says*. London: Faber & Faber.

—(2008), 'World Bookclub – Derek Walcott'. (BBC Podcast), 16 December. Available at: http://www.bbc.co.uk/podcasts/series/wbc#playepisode7

Ward, Abigal. (2007), 'Psychological Formulations' in J. McLeod (ed.), *The Routledge Companion to Postcolonial Studies*. London: Routledge, pp. 190–203.

Watson, Irene. (2009a) 'Sovereign Spaces, Caring for Country and the Homeless Position of Aboriginal Peoples', *South Atlantic Quarterly* 108, (1): 27–51.

—(2009b), 'Aboriginality and the Violence of Colonialism', *Borderlands ejournal* 8 (1). Available at: http://www.borderlands.net.au/vol8no1_2009/iwatson_aboriginality.htm

Weavers, Lydia. (2006), 'Globalising Indigenes: Postcolonial Fiction from Australia, New Zealand and the Pacific', *JASAL* 5: 121–32.

Wenzel, Jennifer. (2006), 'Petro-Magic-Realism: Towards a Political Ecology of Nigerian Literature', *Postcolonial Studies* 9, (4): 449–64.

Williams, Emily Allen. (2000), 'An Interview with Claire Harris', *Wasafiri* 32: 41–4. Williams, Mark. (1997), 'Crippled by Geography? New Zealand Nationalisms' in S. Murray (ed.), *Not on Any Map: Essays on Postcoloniality and Cultural Nationalism*. Exeter: University of Exeter Press, pp. 19–43.

—(2006), 'The Long Maori Renaissance' in Z. Gang, S.L. Gilman and B. Deen Schildgen (eds), *Other Renaissances*. Basingstoke: Palgrave Macmillan, pp. 207–26.

Wolfe, Patrick. (1994), 'Nation and MiscegeNation: Discursive Continuity in the Post-Mabo Era', *Social Analysis* 36: 93–152.

—(2008), 'Structure and Event: Settler Colonialism, Time and the Question of Genocide' in A. Dirk Moses (ed.), *Empire, Colony, Genocide*. New York and Oxford: Berghahn Books, pp. 102–33.

Yeats, W.B. (1902), 'Cathleen Ni Houlihan' in J.P. Harrington (ed.) (1991), *Modern Irish Drama*. New York and London: W.W. Norton & Co., pp. 3–11.

Young, Robert J.C. (1990), *White Mythologies: Writing, History and the West*. London: Routledge.

—(1995), *Colonial Desire: Hybridity in Theory, Culture and Race*. London: Routledge.

—(2001), *Postcolonialism: An Historical Introduction*. Oxford: Blackwell Publishing.

—(2003), *Postcolonialism: A Very Short Introduction*. Oxford: Oxford University Press.

—(2005), 'Fanon and the Turn to Armed Struggle in Africa', *Wasafiri* 44: 33–42.

INDEX

INDEX